CBT
for
Anxiety

A Step-by-Step Training Manual
for the Treatment of Fear, Panic, Worry and OCD

Kimberly J. Morrow, LCSW
Elizabeth DuPont Spencer, LCSW-C

Published by:

PESI Publishing & Media
PESI, Inc
3839 White Ave
Eau Claire, WI 54703

Cover: Amy Rubenzer
Layout: Bookmasters & Amy Rubenzer

ISBN: 9781683731412

Proudly printed in the United States of America

PESI
Publishing
& Media
www.publishing.pesi.com

About the Authors

Kimberly Morrow, LCSW, is a licensed clinical social worker in private practice in Erie, Pennsylvania. A graduate of Memphis State University with a Master's in Psychology and the University of Wisconsin-Milwaukee with a Master's in Social Work, Kimberly has been specializing in treating people with anxiety and OCD for over 25 years and teaching other professionals how to treat anxiety for over 15 years. Kimberly is a graduate of the International Obsessive Compulsive Foundation's Behavior Therapy Institute. She is a member of the National Association of Social Workers and the International Obsessive Compulsive Foundation; a board member of the Obsessive Compulsive Foundation of Western Pennsylvania and an active member of the Anxiety and Depression Association of America, serving on many committees. Kimberly has developed training videos to help clinicians learn evidence-based treatment for anxiety and OCD: http://www.adaa. org/treating-anxiety-disorders-part-1-6-power-anxiety. She is the 2012 recipient of the Clinician Outreach Award and the 2015 Member of Distinction Award from the Anxiety and Depression Association of America. She is the author of *Face It and Feel It: 10 Simple (but Not Easy) Ways to Live Well with Anxiety* (2011).

Elizabeth DuPont Spencer, LCSW-C, is a licensed clinical social worker and Board approved supervisor. Trained as a cognitive behavioral therapist using exposure and response prevention for anxiety disorders, obsessive compulsive disorder, and depression, she has been in private practice for 25 years, working with children, adolescents and adults. Elizabeth is a member of the International Obsessive Compulsive Foundation (IOCDF), the National Association of Social Workers (NASW), and the Anxiety and Depression Association of America (ADAA). She is a Clinical Fellow of the ADAA, and received the 2012 Clinician Outreach Award and the 2017 Member of Distinction Award. Elizabeth is co-owner of AnxietyTraining. com with a mission to train clinicians nation-wide in evidenced-based treatments. A graduate of Columbia University in New York City, and the University of Maryland at the Baltimore's School of Social Work, she completed her clinical training at the National Institutes of Health and the Catholic University of America. She is the co-author of two books, *The Anxiety Cure* and *The Anxiety Cure for Kids*. Elizabeth works in North Bethesda, Maryland.

Dedication

This workbook is dedicated to the millions of people who suffer from anxiety and obsessive compulsive disorder: with successful treatment, you can live a full, rich life. We have shared our best strategies in this workbook so professionals will learn evidence-based treatments to speed your path to wellness.

Acknowledgments

This book exists because many people have helped us along the way. Our editors, Hillary Jenness and Linda Jackson, as well as Meg Graf and Emily Krumenauer, at PESI believed in us from the time they saw us teach our first CBT for Anxiety and OCD webinar. They urged us to extend our work by writing for therapists so they would have easy access to all we teach at our workshops.

Our families have been instrumental in supporting our passion to help as many people as possible who suffer from anxiety and OCD. They have challenged us to reach more people, by training other therapists to do what we love and know works. Thank you to Spence, Greg, and our children for your support and cheerleading to continue forward with this workbook.

We have been humbled by the experiences of our anxious patients and their families who have sought treatment, yet have not been able to find or have access to a therapist who confidently uses cognitive behavior therapy with exposure and response prevention. We have been privileged to work with you and hope, through this workbook, more people will have access to quality care.

This workbook would not exist without our colleagues who study and treat anxiety disorders and OCD and have openly shared their knowledge with us. Challenging each other to come up with better treatments over the past 30 years has been the most exciting way to spend our careers. May we all continue to believe that we can do better and continue to work tirelessly for those who are suffering.

Table of Contents

Introduction

Welcome! We are glad you have found this book, and that you are joining us for our journey as we seek to educate clinicians about cognitive behavioral therapy (CBT) for anxiety disorders and obsessive compulsive disorder (OCD).

Kimberly is from Erie, Pennsylvania, and Elizabeth is from suburban Washington, DC. We each have over 25 years of experience in private practice specializing in treating anxiety and OCD. We found our way to this field through different paths—Elizabeth's sister had anxiety when they were children, and one of Kimberly's first clients had severe, undiagnosed OCD. Along the way, we have each had moments of difficulty with anxiety ourselves. You will learn more about our stories throughout this workbook.

We both find tremendous success for our clients with anxiety and OCD using the treatment outlined in this workbook, and have full private practices with wait lists in our very different practice locations. We know we can help you have a successful practice, too.

We met at the annual conference of the Anxiety and Depression Association of America (ADAA) 10 years ago when we were on the same membership committee. We found a shared passion for educating master's-level clinicians who provide 60% of the mental health care in this country and yet often have little training in evidence-based treatment for anxiety, the most common mental health disorder.

ADAA recently found that it takes on average 33½ years between the time research proves what works to treat anxiety and the time most clinicians are using that knowledge as a standard part of care. We are master's-level clinicians ourselves, and we know that most of us are drawn to this field because we are helpers. We want to help our clients get well from these common and often debilitating mental health disorders. The problem is not in the master's-level clinician, or in the progress being made in the treatment of anxiety and OCD; rather, it is in the lack of access to training. Quite simply, master's-level clinicians have had limited access to learn from the experts in the field.

Our company, AnxietyTraining.com, grew out of our determination to help bridge this gap between what the field knows works and the education most master's-level clinicians receive. Thousands of clinicians across the country and around the world have taken our online training, talked to us via secure video connection for clinical case consultation, or participated in our workshops.

We have worked with community mental health clinics and trained school counselors, as well as worked with clinicians in private practice. What we hear over and over from these clinicians is that, prior to our training, they had not known how to implement CBT for anxiety and OCD. Specifically, clinicians are worried about how to do exposure and response prevention (ERP). We understand! We are all busy, and learning a new skill can seem too difficult while you are seeing clients and managing your personal life. Who has time to go back to school?

Online training, available through PESI, case consultation, available through our website (www.AnxietyTraining. com), and this workbook are all designed to allow you to immediately implement these skills in your practice. Throughout this workbook, we will guide you step-by-step so you know exactly how to do this work. Each chapter follows the same pattern we use with our clients: education, teach a skill, practice the skill, and then homework.

We hope you will pick up a pen and get to work! As we tell our clients, practice is crucial to learn new skills. It takes understanding the concepts and then having an experienced teacher guide you to make using CBT with your clients a strength of your practice. To that end, we have created opportunities in each chapter for clinicians to practice these skills which are labeled, "Your Turn." We want you to find, as so many clinicians we have worked with have found, the power in using these skills with your clients. We want you to feel the pride of having your clients get well and go on to live lives that are not limited by anxiety and OCD.

We hope this workbook is just the beginning of your education. At our website, you can sign up for our monthly email that includes research updates, tips for dealing with specific clinical situations, and links to useful resources. You can also sign up for case consultation or connect with us via email. Once more, welcome. Thank you for joining us.

Chapter 1

Cognitive Behavioral Therapy for Anxiety and OCD

When we began our careers as clinical social workers, we were mystified as to how to help so many different people, from different backgrounds, with different illnesses. How would we ever develop all the skills we needed to make a difference?

Shortly after beginning her career, Kimberly landed a job as an inpatient therapist on a child psychiatric unit. A young girl was admitted who spun herself around in circles over and over again. When Kimberly asked why she did this, she replied that spinning prevented her from looking at her friend's chest and getting feelings that she didn't want to have. This was 25 years ago and at that time we hospitalized her, assuming she was having a psychotic episode. During her stay, it became clear that this girl was wise beyond her years and was clearly in her right mind, but couldn't stop these thoughts or feelings without twirling. She asked Kimberly if anyone else struggled with this and Kimberly set out to discover more. What she learned is that this girl was suffering from obsessive compulsive disorder (OCD). The psychological suffering that this girl endured set Kimberly on a path to discover the best treatments for anxiety and OCD—a form of cognitive behavioral therapy called exposure and response prevention.

Not only did Kimberly find a treatment that was helpful, but she found a treatment that could be used to help a variety of people, from any background, with just about any mental illness.

Cognitive behavioral therapy (CBT) is a structured approach to treatment that has key elements that provide a template for the therapist to use with any client. In this chapter, we will share the principles of CBT, the research that supports it, and key elements for you to understand the foundation of CBT for anxiety and OCD.

FUNDAMENTALS OF COGNITIVE BEHAVIORAL THERAPY

The following ideas create the foundation of cognitive behavioral therapy (Beck, 1995):

- Dysfunctional thinking underlies all emotion and behavior. This is common to all psychological disturbances.

- Challenge your thoughts and change your behavior and you will change your relationship with your emotions.

- Acceptance rather than resistance is the key to improving psychological symptoms.

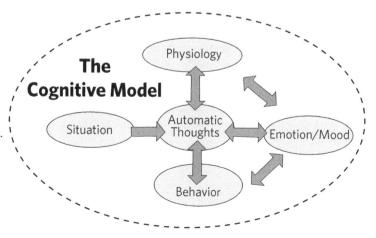

A client came to see Kimberly recently because he had stopped giving presentations at work as he would sweat profusely during these presentations, which led him to develop a fear of people seeing him as incapable of doing his job. He started to come up with reasons not to give the presentations, often asking colleagues if they would pinch hit for him. The more he avoided the presentations, the worse his symptoms became. The sweating began to affect him even when he was talking one-on-one to his colleagues or going out with friends for dinner. He hated the sweating and often thought he would rather just stay home, alone, than deal with these awful feelings.

This is a good example of the role thoughts and behaviors play with emotions and our physiology. The more he avoided, the more anxious he became. The more anxious he became, the more he sweat. The more he resisted, the worse he felt. All of this was heading him in the direction of living a very small life limited by anxiety.

YOUR TURN

Describe a situation where you or a client felt fear.

_____

_____

_____

What symptoms did you feel in your body and where in your body did you feel them?

_____

_____

_____

What did you do to feel better?

_____

_____

_____

Did it work?

_____

_____

_____

What were you thinking during this experience?

_____

_____

_____

Did it help?

_____

_____

_____

What were you feeling before, during, and after this experience?

_____

_____

_____

What happened to these emotions over the course of the experience?

_____

_____

_____

RESEARCH ON COGNITIVE BEHAVIORAL THERAPY

There are over 500 outcome studies on the efficacy of CBT. There are also comprehensive reviews of studies for anxiety and depression from Clark (1999) and Clark and Beck (2010). These studies show the efficacy of CBT for anxiety and depression over the past 30 years. It is important to educate yourself on evidence-based therapies for the illnesses you are treating. CBT has endured as one of the best treatments for anxiety and depression and is helpful in a variety of other diagnoses.

Some of the most exciting research seeks to understand the neurobiological changes in the brain after CBT. A study by Jokić-Begić (2010) demonstrates the neurobiological changes that occur after CBT in patients with arachnophobia, obsessive compulsive disorder, panic disorder, social phobia, major depressive disorder, and chronic fatigue syndrome. One aspect of this study found activation in the right lateral prefrontal cortex (LPFC) and the parahippocampal gyrus with people who had a phobia. After completion of CBT, no significant activation was found in the LPFC and the parahippocampal gyrus. These studies show that CBT treatment may contribute to changes in specific regions of the brain in people suffering from anxiety disorders.

In an article in *The Journal of Clinical Psychiatry* by Otto et al. (2004), cognitive behavioral therapy was found to be helpful in a variety of ways:

- CBT offers long-term maintenance of treatment gains.
- CBT is an effective approach for psychopharmacology nonresponders.
- CBT is a good treatment for those clients who discontinue their medications for anxiety.
- CBT is a good standard treatment to augment pharmacotherapy.

With all that CBT has going for it, how can you afford not to offer it to your clients?

PRINCIPLES OF COGNITIVE BEHAVIORAL THERAPY

Cognitive behavioral therapy has certain principles that are important to learn (Beck, 2011). When working with a client, you will socialize the client about these principles, beginning in the first session. "Socializing" is a CBT term used to educate clients about what to expect in a session. It is an important part of developing a relationship with your client. The more informed the client is on what to expect in a session, the more active they can be in the therapeutic process.

CBT involves collaboration and active participation.

- Therapist and client are a team!
- Client decides what to work on.
- Client identifies their own cognitive distortions.
- Client decides on homework.

CBT starts and spends much time in the present.

- Strong focus on current specific situations that are distressing to them.
- Shift to the past for two reasons:
  ○ If client has a strong need to and it would compromise therapy not to.
  ○ When client gets stuck in dysfunctional thinking and an understanding of where their beliefs come from would be helpful.

CBT includes psychoeducation: teaching the client to be their own therapist.

- Have client take notes in session and bring them home to review/cue throughout week. (In Chapter 4, we will review how to use a notebook in therapy.)

CBT is skills-based.

- Teach and practice skills: inside and outside of session.

CBT involves practice between sessions (homework).

- Throughout the session, identify skills to practice at home.
- This practice will include challenging their automatic thoughts.
- This practice will include changing their behaviors in response to a trigger.
- This practice will include exposing themselves to what they fear (see Chapter 5).

CBT is structured.

- There are different parts of a CBT session that are important to pay attention to so that you can accomplish everything you need to in a session. These include asking about their mood, reviewing homework, setting the agenda, discussing problems, learning and practicing skills in session, developing homework, summarizing the session, and getting feedback from your client.

CBT invites client feedback.

- Giving your clients the chance to give you feedback is important, because research shows we clinicians are not very good judges of our ability. David Burns says we must use measurements with our clients, because our own perceptions may be incorrect: "My research and clinical experience have indicated that this belief may be misguided." (Burns, 2013)

YOUR TURN

It can be anxiety-provoking to ask your clients for feedback. What are your thoughts and feelings? If you don't feel ready to try this now, come back after having read more of this book and see if you feel differently.

_____

_____

_____

_____

_____

_____

CBT Session Structure

Mood check: You can use scales, assessments, inventories, or verbal check in.

Review of week: Ask for highlights of their week. Keep very brief.

Review of homework: Ask about their successes and struggles. Spend time understanding obstacles, cognitive and other, to develop more successful homework.

Set agenda together: Have client give titles to their problems and decide which one is most important to start with today.

Discuss problems related to agenda items: Get into specifics. Use Socratic questions to understand beliefs/rules/assumptions. Have client understand their thoughts related to triggers. Develop new ways to think and new behaviors.

Practice new skills or do in vivo exposure: Practice what they are learning in session.

In vivo exposure is when a person is exposed to situations provoking anxiety in a real-world condition to help them change their relationship with fear and tolerate the accompanying distress. This exposure is done with the therapist.

Set new homework: This is based on what you just talked about. Client decides homework. Discuss their obstacles to doing homework.

Summarize: Client summarizes and writes in their notebook what you discussed.

Feedback: Ask the client to tell you what is helpful and what you could do better.

WORKSHEET

· ·

Client Feedback Form

Name: _____

Date: _____

I welcome your feedback about our session today. Please fill out these questions to help improve our work in the future.

	Disagree			Agree	
I felt that my therapist understood me today	1	2	3	4	5
My therapist is a warm, caring person	1	2	3	4	5
We worked on topics we both agreed on	1	2	3	4	5
We set goals together	1	2	3	4	5
Therapy is helping me get better	1	2	3	4	5
I plan to do the homework we agreed on	1	2	3	4	5

Comments:

_____

_____

_____

YOUR TURN

Write a script for yourself of how you might socialize your client to cognitive behavioral therapy (be sure to include what CBT is; the importance of being a team; what they can expect during a session, including homework; and your desire for feedback).

_____

_____

_____

_____

_____

_____

CONNECTING THOUGHTS AND FEELINGS

As explained in the fundamentals of CBT, it is important to help clients connect their thoughts and feelings. Often, when we ask someone how they feel about something, they may respond with what they were thinking or what they did about the situation. Similarly, if you ask what they were thinking, they may respond with how they were feeling. To help connect thoughts and feelings, you can start with a discussion about how they view the connection between thoughts, feelings, and behaviors.

Asking them to keep track of what they are thinking when they notice an increase in anxiety can be helpful with this connection. Give them this assignment as part of their homework.

They can also write down triggers, thoughts, feelings, and behavioral responses to help them see the connection.

YOUR TURN

How do you view the connection between thoughts and feelings? Which seems more powerful to you? Are you aware of both your thoughts and feelings in trigger situations?

_____

_____

_____

Think of an anxiety-provoking situation you have recently experienced. How did you know it was anxiety-provoking?

_____

_____

_____

What were you thinking during that situation?

_____

_____

_____

How did you respond to the anxiety in that situation?

_____

_____

_____

Finally, asking Socratic questions can be very helpful to this discussion with your client. Socratic questioning involves engaging the person in critical thinking. This enables your client to process their thoughts and feelings related to a situation. Anxiety is clever at convincing us that things are a certain way, are fixed, and are unchangeable. Socratic questioning can challenge those assumptions/beliefs and help us come up with more realistic possibilities. Socratic questioning also takes the pressure off you and allows the client to develop a keener sense of the connection between their thoughts and feelings. See the following handout for examples.

Socratic Questions

Conceptual clarification questions

- Why are you saying that?
- What exactly does this mean?
- How does this relate to what we have been talking about?
- What is the nature of ...?
- What do we already know about this?
- Can you give me an example?
- Are you saying ... or ...?

Probing assumptions

- What else could we assume?
- You seem to be assuming...?
- Why did you choose that assumption?
- What evidence do you have that your assumption is true?
- What would happen if ...?

Probing rationale, reasons, and evidence

- Why is that happening?
- How do you know this?
- Show me ...
- Can you give me an example of that?
- What do you think causes ...?
- What is the nature of this?

Questioning viewpoints and perspectives

- Another way of looking at this is ... Does this seem reasonable?
- What alternative ways of looking at this are there?
- Why is ... necessary?
- Who benefits from this?
- What is the difference between ... and ...?
- Why is it better than ...?

Probing implications and consequences

- ° Then what would happen?
- ° What are the consequences of that assumption?
- ° How could ... be used to ...?
- ° What are the implications of ...?
- ° How does ... affect ...?
- ° How does ... fit with what we learned before?
- ° Why is ... important?

INTERRUPTING

Often, anxious clients feel compelled to share their anxiety stories with you and anyone who will listen. They believe this helps because it feels better to tell someone and they often get some form of reassurance. As you will learn in Chapter 4, both of these responses will only serve to perpetuate anxiety in the long run.

After compassionately listening and validating their distress, it can be helpful to use interrupting as a method to bring the conversation back to the task at hand: developing healthier behavioral and cognitive responses to their anxious feelings. Many clinicians are reluctant to interrupt because they don't want to be disrespectful. It is important to socialize your client to this early on in treatment, saying something like, "Sharing your experiences with me is important. I hope that we can both learn more about your patterns with anxiety. However, there are times that I will gently hold my hand up to interrupt a story you are telling me. The reason I am doing this is so that we don't connect and reinforce your anxiety circuit. It is also important that we leave enough time in our session to practice the skills you are learning."

YOUR TURN

Using interrupting, practice responding to a client who has been telling you about a vacation they took, giving many details where they felt panic symptoms during both the flight and driving to different locations.

_____

_____

_____

_____

_____

_____

_____

_____

COGNITIVE BEHAVIORAL THERAPY FOR ANXIETY: WHAT'S DIFFERENT

There are a few important distinctions when using cognitive behavioral therapy for anxiety and for obsessive compulsive disorder as opposed to other disorders. These will be discussed more thoroughly throughout this workbook.

- Exposure and response prevention (ERP): This is the hallmark of CBT for both anxiety and OCD. It involves exposing yourself to the things that you fear. ERP involves developing a trigger list of things you fear and then rank ordering that list from least anxiety-provoking to most anxiety-provoking. The least anxiety-provoking trigger is then used to develop an exposure where the client practices facing their fear and learning how to have a healthier response to their thoughts and feelings.
- Challenging cognitions is the other important piece of CBT for both anxiety and OCD. However, this differs from treating other disorders in two important ways:
  - Instead of coming up with positive ways to think about the situation, you will be teaching them how to see the situation realistically. They will also need to learn healthy self-talk to help them ride the wave of anxiety they are experiencing.
  - Instead of finding ways to avoid or get rid of their anxious feelings, they will need to practice accepting their feelings and continuing to do whatever they were doing before the anxiety surfaced.

WHAT IS NOT HELPFUL

There are some approaches to CBT for anxiety and OCD that have been found to be unhelpful.

- Reassurance: Giving reassurance to the client to help them feel better during an anxiety-provoking situation teaches them and their brain that they are not capable of handling the feeling and actually serves to strengthen the anxiety connection.

- Distraction: This is not helpful for the same reasons that reassurance is not helpful. A person needs to be able to face their feelings and tolerate them to create new brain connections. Distraction only serves to teach the brain that they cannot handle the feelings.

- Relaxation techniques: Mindfulness, meditation, and relaxation techniques are essential to living well with anxiety. However, using relaxation techniques during an episode of anxiety or OCD prevents the person from developing an approach to handling the feeling. It also only serves to strengthen the anxiety connection when used inappropriately.

RELAPSE PREVENTION

The goal of therapy is to have remission of symptoms and for the person to have developed skills to use for future problem-solving. We often tell people that their goal is to work us out of a job. To set your clients up for success, there are some important things to remember.

- Prepare client early: At first session, socialize client into a time-limited treatment.
- When client begins to feel better, discuss course of recovery: improvement-plateaus-setbacks.
- Always attribute progress at every session to the client.
- Role-play potential new symptoms and how they would use their new CBT skills to manage these symptoms.

CONCLUSION

You may be wondering what happened to that girl who was hospitalized for spinning around for fear of having unpleasant thoughts and feelings. A few years ago, this same young lady—who was now a college student in Kimberly's husband's class—came up to him and asked if he was Kimberly's husband. He said yes. She told him that she had been Kimberly's client many years ago and wanted to thank her for the treatment she eventually received, which was CBT with exposure and response prevention. She wanted Kimberly to know that she was doing well.

Chapter Highlights

- Cognitive behavioral therapy is a well-researched treatment that is effective for anxiety and OCD.
- Challenge thoughts and change behaviors, and the relationship with fear changes.
- Use Socratic questions to help connect feelings and thoughts.
- Exposure and response prevention (ERP) is important in CBT for anxiety and OCD.
- Challenge automatic thoughts with rational and realistic thoughts, not positive ones.
- Interrupting can be helpful to you and your client in a CBT session.
- Do not reassure or teach distraction or relaxation when using exposure therapy.
- Prepare for termination by attributing success to client.

TAKE THE NEXT STEP

Think about why you purchased this workbook. Record your responses to the following questions:

Who are you hoping to help?

_____

_____

_____

Why did you think this book would be helpful to you?

_____

_____

_____

Do you believe that changing the way you think about anxiety and changing how you respond to a trigger can affect how you feel about something?

_____

_____

_____

How do you feel about engaging in exposure and response prevention with clients?

_____

_____

_____

Chapter 2

Assessment and Diagnosis of Anxiety and OCD

We feel excited every time we have a session with a new client. It's an adventure, and, much like travel, the adventure of learning about a new person energizes us. Even though we've seen thousands of new clients in our 25 years providing CBT for people of all ages with anxiety and OCD, each story is different in important ways.

Part of the excitement comes from knowing that the process of assessment and diagnosis of anxiety and OCD is a crucial step in reaching the goal of helping people live full lives. Being able to help people understand what is wrong and give them a name for the suffering they are experiencing is powerful: with the right diagnosis, it is possible for you and your client to select the best treatment and connect with resources online. Keep in mind that it takes on average 14–17 years for someone with OCD to get the right diagnosis. Your clinical knowledge is very important. You are a team doing this work—they are the expert in their specific problem, and you are the expert in CBT for anxiety and OCD (Szymanski, 2012).

ELIZABETH'S STORY

While we each have been working as clinicians for 25 years, Elizabeth's experience with anxiety goes back to her childhood and the terrible claustrophobia her younger sister experienced in first grade. At that time, children were not thought to experience anxiety disorders—hard as that is to imagine now.

The year before the claustrophobia took over her sister and their whole family, the two sisters had been at a friend's house playing hide and seek, and were briefly stuck in a closet. Elizabeth remembers the experience—the way the dust drifted in the shaft of light that shone under the door, and the way her younger sister shivered with fear. Elizabeth tried to comfort her, confident that they would be found quickly, and it seemed to her that they were. However, the following year, the first-grade classroom her sister was in had an attached bathroom without windows, and she would not use it. Being a helpful sister, Elizabeth worked out a plan that she would meet her at recess and hold the door for her so she could use a different restroom.

This worked well enough, but the problems quickly began to multiply. Elizabeth's sister would no longer go in elevators, and then stairwells that had doors at the bottom and top quickly became off-limits. Going to school became a torture as their mother drove them to school and walked Elizabeth's sobbing sister to her classroom. Elizabeth was in third grade, and felt horrified and mystified by the problem. Her father, a psychiatrist, was equally mystified, but he found a newly-opened treatment program at the Phobia Center in White Plains, New York, and he went from their home outside of Washington, DC, to New York to get training in this new treatment, Contextual Therapy.

Contextual therapy was an early form of CBT. When he came home, he explained that Elizabeth's sister's brain was sending the wrong signals, and that she would need to gradually practice the things she was fearful of to get better. The two of them started to practice together, and she eventually recovered fully from the grip of the claustrophobia that felt like it had threatened to engulf the whole family.

ACTING ODDLY

People with anxiety don't always act in polite or reasonable ways, as illustrated by the example with Elizabeth's otherwise sweet sister and her temper tantrums due to anxiety when she was dropped off at school. As a clinician, it is essential to be a nice person to your client. Meet their anxiety, which may be expressed as defiance or humiliation, with understanding and compassion. You are not saying the anxiety is right or true, but you are validating the difficult experience they are having.

Empathy increases trust between clinician and client and it improves treatment outcome as well (Hara et al., 2016). Empathy can be conveyed to a client through verbal and nonverbal communication. While empathy alone will not solve the problems with anxiety and OCD, it is extremely important to building an alliance that will allow you to work with very anxious clients. Empathy and being a warm, kind person are so important to all the work you will do with your anxious client (Teding van Berkhout & Malouff, 2016).

EMPATHY-BUILDERS

- Being present with our clients in the moment is crucial, though sometimes painful.
- Use reflective listening to be sure you clearly understand what they are saying.
- Display interest in what the client is saying—nod, smile, frown appropriately.
- Let the client see your emotions about what they are saying—be genuine.
- Try to see things as your client sees them.

A first session is a huge leap of faith for a person with anxiety. They are telling about terribly personal and painful parts of their lives, things they often have never told another person. The very best thing you can do for an anxious person is to treat what they say with the respect it deserves. They may talk about obsessions that are disturbing or odd, or about fears that are illogical or impossible.

Elizabeth remembers her first session with Jennifer, who was seven, and her mother. Both were completely freaked out. The week before, her mother had taken her to the gas station on an errand to fill up the car. As her mother pumped the gas, Jennifer began screaming from her booster seat. Her mother rushed to her side, and found Jennifer sobbing that she had swallowed gasoline. Nothing her mother said calmed her. They returned home and Jennifer insisted on washing all her clothes and taking a bath, and would not eat dinner. The next day things were calmer, but when Jennifer's mother made a small comment about the day before, Jennifer again began screaming. This continued for another day, until Jennifer's mother helped her zip up her jacket to go to school, and Jennifer began yelling that she had swallowed her zipper. The two of them looked terrified as they told me this story, and Jennifer's mother looked guilty as well, perhaps fearing this problem reflected on her ability as a mother.

Think about what you can say with compassion and empathy:

- I can hear how much you have been suffering with this.
- I'm so glad you chose to come see me to talk about this.
- There is effective treatment for this problem.
- I can see this is harming your life.
- What a difficult situation.

Jennifer was suffering from OCD. Her odd symptoms and fears are some of the type that younger children with OCD often exhibit. OCD has two clusters of ages of onset: 5–8 years and adolescence. At seven years old, Jennifer fit right in with the timing of the onset of her illness, and one of the most important parts of treatment was giving her and her mother the name for what the problem was.

Consider your intake forms. As you sit with a new client, you need basic information from them. Intake forms are the first contact your clients have with you. Having a questionnaire that asks about anxiety, depression, and OCD symptoms goes a long way to helping your client recognize that they are in the right place with a clinician who understands what their problem is. You can find a number of these online, but we find simple forms work well for us, and have included them on the following pages.

There are a few problems that can mimic anxiety disorders. Be sure you ask your client about their use of caffeine, alcohol, and drug abuse or over-the-counter medicines, and check to see if they have had a physical exam and blood work to rule out thyroid disorders. For children with a sudden onset of OCD symptoms, make sure they are fully evaluated for PANS (pediatric acute-onset neuropsychiatric syndrome), which can occur after strep or other viruses.

The DSM-5® has a system of free, age-specific crosscutting measurements that are very helpful for getting to some of the distinctions between different anxiety disorders. You can use a Level 1 measure to get a general idea about the focus of the problem, and the answers the client gives will help guide you to a Level 3 measurement.

Many therapists who are not familiar with using the DSM-5® struggle with how to visualize what a specific phobia looks like. For example, how would you sort out body dysmorphia from OCD? Having a copy of the DSM-5 or looking online is a great help, and becoming familiar with where to find the diagnostic information will serve you well when you get a confounding case—people don't always fit neatly into particular categories!

The following exercises are meant to help you look for identifying information in a client's story and use that to find an appropriate diagnosis.

···

Anxiety, OCD and Depression Screening

Name: _____   Date: _____

Please circle the response that best describes you. Feel free to change the wording of a particular question to fit your situation.

0 = Not at all true   1= Somewhat true   2 = Moderately true
3 = Very true   4 = Completely true

1. I worry a lot of the time	0	1	2	3	4
2. I often feel depressed and down	0	1	2	3	4
3. I have panic or anxiety attacks	0	1	2	3	4
4. There are places I avoid	0	1	2	3	4
5. I am shy and nervous with people	0	1	2	3	4
6. My anxiety is embarrassing	0	1	2	3	4
7. I have bad/upsetting thoughts	0	1	2	3	4
8. I have to do things just so or over and over	0	1	2	3	4
9. I experience frequent pain	0	1	2	3	4
10. My sleep is a problem	0	1	2	3	4
11. My difficulties impact work or school	0	1	2	3	4
12. My family and friends notice my difficulty	0	1	2	3	4

What is the main problem you are having?

_____

_____

_____

In order to conclude that your treatment was successful, what would you want to achieve?

_____

_____

_____

....

Evaluating the Anxiety, OCD and Depression Screening

Questions below correspond to the screening questions on page 20. Circle all that are present for this client. Double circle all 3 and 4 answers

Question Number	Possible Diagnosis
1.	GAD or phobias
2.	Depression
3.	Panic disorder
4.	Phobia, phobia or OCD
5.	Social Anxiety Disorder
6.	Social Anxiety Disorder
7.	OCD
8.	OCD
9.	A frequent complication of anxiety, OCD and depression
10.	A frequent complication of anxiety, OCD and depression
11.	Screen for severity of the impact of anxiety, OCD and depression
12.	Screen for severity of the impact of anxiety, OCD and depression

....

Questions to Ask a Client at a First Visit

1. What is the main problem that is bothering you?

2. When did it start / how long has it been going on?

3. Was anything new or stressful going in your life at the time?

4. Do you drink beverages with caffeine or use drugs recreationally?

5. Has your problem been the same since it started, or has it changed?

6. Have you had a physical exam recently and blood work to test for thyroid problems?

7. Can you give me some examples of what you are worrying about or what you avoid?

8. How is your life impacted now by this problem?

9. What things can you not do or do you miss out on due to this problem?

10. Does anything help to make it better?

11. How do other people help you when you are experiencing anxiety?

CLINICIAN EXERCISE

Anxiety Disorder Assessement

Read the following stories, and then draw a line between the client and the diagnosis in the box below. Answers can be found on page 25.

Client	Diagnosis Choices
Lisa	Separation anxiety disorder F93.0
Thomas	Body dysmorphic disorder F45.22
Jennifer	Specific phobia F40.9
Caroline	Selective mutism F94.0
Joe	Panic disorder F41.0
Jenny	OCD F42.9
Justin	Agoraphobia F40.0
Clayton	Social anxiety disorder F40.1

Stories:

Lisa, a second-grade student, will not speak in school. In kindergarten and first grade, she did not speak, but because she did not cause trouble and did all of her homework correctly, her teachers did not find it to be a problem. Now, in second grade, her teacher wants her to participate and wants a plan of communication. Lisa talks a lot at home with her parents and sister but, even with other family members, she will not talk. Her grandmother recently told her mother that it was shameful that her granddaughter would not say hello to her at her birthday party.

Thomas, a bright-eyed, energetic 12-year-old, was walking with his mother in the supermarket parking lot. He saw a dog on a leash approaching. Fast as lightning, he ran into the street and was narrowly missed by a car. He won't go to the houses of any friends or relatives who have dogs. But this was the first time he had done anything like this.

Jennifer is a beautiful, stylish, 20-year-old young woman. Her father died suddenly when she was five years old and, after that, her mother homeschooled her. Jennifer and her mother are close, and they can't go anywhere without the other one. For two years, Jennifer has attended community college courses while her mother stays waiting for her in the parking lot. Jennifer has now graduated from community college, and her mom does not want to continue waiting in the parking lot after the hour-long drive to the college Jennifer wants to attend. Jennifer feels terrified by the idea of having to make the drive and be away from her mother while she attends classes at this new school.

Caroline is 21, beautifully dressed and poised in my office. She is home from college on medical leave, taking a semester off. She has always been shy and struggled to communicate with others, but last semester she broke up with her boyfriend and struggled in a class for the very first time in her life. During that time, other students saw her crying and disheveled. Caroline feels totally humiliated and exposed. Because people saw her weakness, she can't face going back to school.

Joe is a 17-year-old with autism who wants to wear a mask to school because he does not want anyone to see his mouth or his nose, which he feels are deformed. Joe now sits in the back of the class turned away from other students so no one can see his face. He spends hours in the bathroom looking in the mirror, finding horrible deformities in his appearance.

Jenny is a serious, slightly heavy 28-year-old who is engaged to a very kind and loving man. Jenny traveled extensively with her parents as a teenager, but now she cannot fly or drive distances from home, and she can't stay at hotels. Jenny's wedding is in three weeks and the venue is an hour and a half away. When she planned the wedding last year, it was fine, but now she cannot get herself to go. She is afraid she will miss her own wedding, though she is very excited to be married.

Justin is 15. His hands are red and chapped because he washes them over and over in very hot water. He is distressed about touching things because he is worried about germs. During his first therapy session, he holds his hands clasped in his lap, not touching the chair. He says "I love you, Mom" over and over, needing to have his mom say "I love you, Joe" back every time.

Clayton is 22 and fiercely proud of his independence. He did not go to college but has a skilled job as an auto mechanic and is making much better money than his peers who went to college. He wears his hair long and has tattoos on both forearms. Clayton had a sudden attack of dizziness and fear in high school, and though the attacks came only a few times in his senior year, they are part of why he decided not to go to college. He associates the attacks with being in places he cannot leave easily. Recently he was supposed to go to the dentist for his annual cleaning and realized that was another place he would be stuck if he had an attack. After that, he realized that though he wanted to get a haircut, this would be another place he would be stuck because he couldn't leave in the middle of a shampoo. The attacks are occurring more frequently, and Clayton is terrified that they will begin to interfere with work. He already had to take several sick days to stay home when he feared he might have an attack.

ASSESSMENT OF OCD

There are a couple of helpful assessment tools that you can use for working with a client that you suspect has obsessive compulsive disorder. Jonathon Grayson has helpful assessment tools on his website www.freedomfromocd.com. The Yale-Brown Obsessive Compulsive Scale (YBOCS) can be filled out with your client in the office or can be given to them to take home. It allows you to ask them about typical obsessions and compulsions. They check which ones they have currently and which they have had in the past. It also has a scale that allows you to identify the severity of their symptoms from 0–40. Our goal is to have people be below 15 on the YBOCS severity rating scale by the end of therapy. A client that is above 20 may benefit from a medication; consult before beginning ERP.

Chapter Highlights

- Getting the right diagnosis requires collaboration with your client.
- Empathy and validation are crucial to understanding the problem.
- Goal is to have the client leave with hope.
- Use crosscutting measurements to make distinctions between anxiety disorders.
- Review the diagnostic criteria for the diagnoses you use most frequently.

TAKE THE NEXT STEP

Review your intake forms and consider adding a checklist or inventory to capture client anxiety and depression. See reference section for suggestions.

ANSWERS TO ANXIETY DISORDER ASSESSMENT

Jennifer—Separation anxiety disorder—F93.0

Joe—Body dysmorphic disorder F45.22

Thomas—Specific phobia F40.9

Lisa—Selective mutism F94.0

Clayton—Panic disorder F41.0

Justin—OCD F42.9

Jenny—Agoraphobia F40.0

Caroline—Social anxiety disorder F40.1

Chapter 3

Being a Team and Setting Goals with Your Clients

Our clients come to see us feeling overwhelmed by anxiety and OCD. Anxiety typically has them avoiding triggers and therefore missing important parts of their lives and suffering terribly. It's also easy for clinicians to get overwhelmed as we get to know our clients.

Elizabeth saw a client a few years ago. James, who was 55, came to see her having been referred by his primary-care doctor. James had been riding the subway home from work in Washington, DC, when he was overwhelmed by a feeling that he was having a heart attack. He stumbled out of the station and collapsed outside the entrance, where an ambulance was called and he was taken to the hospital. Elizabeth met James two days later, after he had been cleared of having any medical problems. James was still stunned by what had happened and worried the doctors had missed something.

James was gingerly feeling his chest and squeezing his left arm to check to see if he had a shooting pain. He had not been back to work and had not been exercising, sleeping, or eating much. The day before the incident on the subway, he had returned from an urgent visit to his son who was in college in another state. His son had just broken up with his girlfriend and was struggling to get out of bed and go to classes. This had been terribly upsetting for James to see.

Additionally, James said that he had concerns about his finances. His wife was very upset that he was so stressed, and she spent a lot of time reassuring him that his son, his health, and his finances were going to be okay.

We are using James as an example because Elizabeth well remembers how she felt as he told his story and she reviewed his anxiety evaluation forms. She quickly caught the feeling of being overwhelmed from him. Her thought was, "I have so much I need to help him with, and we need to get him back to work and able to travel quickly because he also has financial pressures. I need to make sure he understands everything right now."

This sense of urgency and responsibility is very common in therapists. We are helpers, and seeing someone who is overwhelmed and in pain makes us feel like getting to work! The problem here was that even though she was pretty sure the diagnosis was panic disorder, James was not seeing things that way at all. He was still lost in the topics of his fears about a health problem, his son, and his finances, and what he knew helped was his wife's reassurance. You see how he and Elizabeth were in no position to collaborate:

	Elizabeth's Perspective	**James's Perspective**
Problem	Panic disorder	Health, son, finances
Next Step	Self-care, exposure	A doctor; reassurance; work
Time Frame	Session next week	Need help right now!

USING A NOTEBOOK

James and Elizabeth had to get onto the same page to work together. She reached over to a pile of spiral notebooks and passed him one. Using a notebook with clients feels like magic. James is a great example of how well this works.

Elizabeth explained to him that they had to be really thoughtful about what the problem was right then. Having the notebook in his hands seemed to wake him up from the anxious daze he had been locked in. He picked up a pen and got to work. They started where we always start—what is the problem right now? He listed the three topics he had—health, son, finances. Elizabeth suggested he might add the incident that had occurred on the subway, since he had medical testing to show it was not a heart attack. He liked adding to his list!

Then she read him the definition of a panic attack from the DSM-5 and he agreed it sounded like what had happened to him, so he added some notes about how to define a panic attack. This felt like enormous progress, because he had acknowledged panic was a part of the problem. Finding that one area of agreement to begin their collaboration was the pivot they needed to move forward. The remarkable thing about this story is that James saw Elizabeth for only six sessions, and then he was done with therapy. He had learned how to be his own therapist and his wife had learned how to be his coach instead of providing the continual accommodation she had prior to therapy.

YOUR TURN

Do you like the idea of having clients use a notebook? Why or why not?

_____

_____

_____

The collaboration approach to CBT means that it is essential to start your client taking notes early on in this process. During a first session, once they have told us something about what brought them to a therapist's office, have filled out evaluation paperwork, and we have a working diagnosis, then ask them to keep track of what we are saying because it is very important information.

NOTEBOOK STRATEGIES

Elizabeth hands every client a spiral notebook from the pile she has in her office, and asks them to start by writing a few lines on the first page, which we title "My Anxiety History." Most people can write two or three lines while we are together, and children draw a picture. Some people take this home for homework if they have a lot of details they want to record; for example, if they have multiple experiences with therapists or many trials on medication. Every week, clients fill out logs or record homework in the notebook, and bring it back to sessions so we can continue to record our work together.

Say to your client, "You are the expert in your anxiety and this notebook is going to help you show me what is difficult in your life. Using a notebook allows you to connect what we are doing in a session to what you are experiencing in your life, and to bring things from life back to our sessions. It magnifies the effect of the time we have together. It is also going to help me teach you a new way of looking at the problem. You will be able to record your work outside of our sessions and bring the record back to show me what worked and what didn't work, so we can work together to help you be more and more successful over time."

Sometimes clients are reluctant to use a notebook. "It's too old-fashioned," "I don't like to write," "I'll just forget to bring it," are some standard reasons clients give when presented with a notebook. We get it! They have just met us, and we are asking them to write something that, in one way or another, is making them more anxious. We usually gently push the client to give it a try by saying, "Well, keeping track of what you are learning in here and what you try outside of our appointments is very helpful to most people. What about trying it for a week and let me know how it goes?" If they refuse at that point, move on. When you and your client come up with a homework assignment at the end of the session, try a Socratic question, "I can see it might be hard to keep track of that assignment. Do you have any thoughts about how you might help yourself remember it?" Some clients do well using a note or reminder on their phone so if they suggest that, give it a try. As with all therapy, no one way works for everyone.

The notebooks can be very useful throughout therapy and beyond. We think of two 8-year-old boys. One used the notebook in our first two sessions, and then his mother forgot it at home saying dismissively, "Well, it wasn't very useful, anyway." By the fourth session, the child was in tears because he could remember specific things we had done in our sessions, but could not remember how they connected to his anxiety. His mother brought the notebook back in the fifth session, and the child and therapist happily told the story of his anxiety and looked at the pictures and charts they had created. The child made huge improvements after that and was soon done with therapy.

The other boy came in for three sessions, quickly improved, and was done with therapy, which sometimes happens with children. A year later, a new trigger brought the anxiety back and he came back for a few more sessions. He had his notebook, and he and his therapist could quickly review what he had learned so successfully, helping move him forward quickly again.

Some therapists prefer to have clients use a series of handouts or note cards, and we have made sample pages throughout this workbook to use however you find useful. These sample pages work either way—have your client copy the chart or question into a notebook, or hand them a page with the chart or question to fill out for next session. No one can get better from anxiety without exposure to the feared situation or topic, and homework is the way that you and your client can calibrate the pace and success of the work.

It's important to remember that our brains can have a negative bias, which causes us to over-focus on problems or difficulties and under-focus on successes. This is very common with anxiety and leads the client to constantly over-attend to the problems that still exist with anxiety and under-attend to the progress they have made. We like to say the journey up the mountain to leading a full, successful life starts with one footstep, but feels dwarfed by the mountain and can lead people to give up when they are really on the road to success. Recording the steps along the way is a wonderful antidote to this problem, as clients can see in their own writing the progress that they are making.

CBT always involves homework, and research shows that clients who do homework get on average 10% better than those who don't do homework. As clinicians, we want that extra 10% improvement for our clients, and getting them to take ownership for a record of their work is a good way to get them started early on in treatment. Also, we like to remind our clients that our goal is to work ourselves out of a job by helping them learn to be their own therapist, and we do that by having them write their own self-help book (LeBeau, Davies, Culver, & Craske, 2013).

When you work with a child or someone who has a family member with them, put a Post-it Note as a flag about 10 pages from the back of the notebook and label it "Parent Section." This is where you will give the parents assignments, including the Coaching Tips (see Chapter 6). It's also a place to help take the pressure off the parent and child who are likely struggling at home about the symptoms of anxiety. If parent and child argue about whether something is anxiety or not, ask the parent not to struggle, but to simply record the incident in the notebook. Family members play an important role in getting well from anxiety. Having a place for them to record questions or homework in the notebook includes the loved ones right from the beginning of therapy.

Writing down homework is a simple, powerful CBT technique, and most people love this collaborative work. Yet some of the clients that we see refuse to write things down. They see it as too old-school because no technology is involved. We have explored apps with clients who have this feeling, and there are several that are helpful, but nothing is as flexible and perfectly personalizable as a notebook. Sure, a few of our clients successfully use the notes feature on their phones to keep these records, but there's not much space to work with, and we can't draw the pictures and keep the charts that we find so helpful.

It's useful to know that research shows that clients don't need to believe that therapy will work. I tell them to "fake it til they make it." Also, it is important to let them know that practicing their homework is one of the most important parts of therapy as that is what teaches their brain to make healthier connections when their anxiety is triggered.

Clients who refuse to do work between sessions are missing a big part of the benefit of the work. Think about what you want to say to clients who do not do homework. We take a "three strikes and you are out" position—if you don't do homework three times, you need to stop seeing us for three months. At that point, you can try again if you feel ready to do the work.

USING AN ANXIETY SCALE:
SUBJECTIVE UNITS OF DISTRESS SCALE (SUDS)

Anxiety isn't just present or absent: it exists on a continuum. Ask clients to rate their anxiety. The SUDS can be used to measure anxiety as a way of helping you and your client determine how much anxiety they are experiencing from a trigger and during an exposure. The units go from 0–10, where 0 is a breeze and 10 is a panic attack. Ask clients to rate their anxiety triggers on a scale of 0-10 at the start of treatment. SUDS can also be used to assess a client's level of anxiety during an exposure. You can use this scale to determine which trigger to begin with when you move to Chapter 5, The Art of Exposure and Response Prevention (Wolpe & Joseph, 1969).

DEVELOPING TRIGGER LISTS

It is important for you and your client to develop a list of what triggers them, how much anxiety they experience during the trigger, and what their response is to the trigger. You will use this list to develop their exposures. The anxiety levels will help determine which trigger to face first.

Always begin with the lowest anxiety level, so that they can practice good exposure skills with success before moving on to more anxiety-provoking situations. The list of what they do to feel better before they start treatment will be helpful to identify safety behavior. The goal is not to engage in any of these behaviors while they are practicing an exposure. It is also important to understand what their family and friends do to help them when their anxiety is triggered. In Chapter 6, you will learn how to educate family and friends to be coaches, so that they can be a part of the solution.

Let's look at a trigger list for James:

Trigger	SUDS
Riding the metro	10
Feeling his heart beat strongly	9
Receiving a phone call from his son	9
Looking at his bank statement	8
Exercising	6
Eating a full meal	6

Notice how nothing in his life was less than a 6—even things like eating and exercising were causing him distress. James had become highly sensitized to how his body felt, and because he was monitoring every feeling, he found that each feeling was strange and fearful. Not eating or sleeping much had clearly made this whole situation worse.

Writing this all down gave James a bit of perspective on his situation, and he recognized that it was going to be important for him to track his anxiety triggers over the next week because he found they were changing rapidly. He also saw that returning to a more usual, though gentler, schedule would be helpful, and decided to go for a walk with his wife every day, eat three meals a day, and get to bed by midnight. He wrote his homework in his notebook:

1. Fill out trigger chart and record SUDS levels.
2. Read the ADAA website page about panic disorder and share that with his wife.
3. Walk every day.
4. Eat three light meals a day.
5. Get to bed by midnight.

Before they wrapped up their session, Elizabeth asked James to briefly outline some goals. This is not going to be our only time to consider goals, but clients sometimes get better so fast that capturing the goals they have when they first arrive for treatment can be important in helping the client see their progress. James's goals:

Easy—Eat three meals a day; walk every day; go to bed by midnight.

Medium—Return to work; read a bank statement.

Hard—Eat a Thanksgiving-sized meal; play a sport strenuously.

Impossible—Ride the subway.

This was a tremendous start for a client who, at the beginning of the session, had been unable to identify what the problem was or how to begin to get well. Elizabeth and James did the work together, and they used the strength of CBT to set up their work. James left with a feeling of direction and an idea of what he could do prior to their next session.

YOUR TURN

- Make a list of things that trigger something you fear, along with your anxiety level and what you do to feel better.
- Now go back and rank order your triggers from least anxiety-provoking to most anxiety-provoking.

Trigger List			
Ranking	Trigger situation	SUDS (0–10)	What I do to feel better

Using a Notebook to Increase Homework Compliance—*Sample Topics*

Following is an example of the information we ask clients to document in their notebook.

1. My Anxiety History

2. Why Try CBT?

3. My Diagnosis

4. The Problems Anxiety Causes in My Life

5. What My Life Would Look Like If I Didn't Have Anxiety

6. Make an anxiety scale/SUDS scale 0-10

7. Set early goals—Easy, Medium, and Hard or Impossible

8. Pick a homework assignment, which usually involves tracking anxiety levels or triggers

Chapter Highlights

- Have your client use a notebook or note cards to increase motivation and homework compliance.
- Introduce an anxiety scale 0–10.
- Develop a SUDS hierarchy.

TAKE THE NEXT STEP

Incorporate the use of a notebook or note cards in your practice with one client. How did it go?

_____

_____

_____

_____

Chapter 4

Helping Your Clients Understand Their Anxious Brains

Clients with anxiety are all different and unique—even two people with fear of elevators will need different things in their treatment from you. Yet everyone who has an anxiety disorder has a brain-based problem that is causing them tremendous suffering. Once you have a diagnosis, you continue your journey with your client by helping them to understand their anxious brain. I know that many clinicians will want to skip this chapter, fearing it is too complicated. Clients want to skip this, too! Give it a try, even though you might feel intimidated. This is a great opportunity to face your fear and do it anyway. Understanding and being able to teach our clients about the anxious brain is powerful CBT.

CASE EXAMPLE

Ralph was a 20-year-old college sophomore when he came in for a first session with Elizabeth. He was home from college after a disastrous fall semester, and we knew we would only have four sessions before he would return to college. Freshman year had gone relatively well for him because he had immediately become best friends with his roommate.

Though the two of them had different classes and majors, they spent most of their time together and neither one made any other close friends. At the end of the year, as they were set to pick housing together, his roommate surprised him by saying he was dropping out of college. This meant that Ralph, with no back-up plan for housing, was put into a quad room with three people he did not know who all turned out to be members of the lacrosse team. Isolated and unhappy with his major, Ralph nearly failed his fall classes, and was on academic probation when I saw him.

Once I concluded he had social anxiety disorder and came up with a trigger list and early goals, I showed Ralph how to draw a brain, and used the drawing to explain the stuck situation he was in. It's impossible to convey the power of these simple psychoeducational interventions. Not only did he have a name for the isolation and suffering he was experiencing, he had an image of what was wrong with his brain. This helped him understand that he was not making up his symptoms and that his brain could get rewired.

BRAIN EVOLUTION

Our brains developed the structure they have today back when we were primitive humans living in small tribes as hunter-gatherers. We were nomadic, following the seasons and food supply. It's amazing to imagine our primitive ancestors who had nothing more than we have in our bodies and brains, and yet they survived the ice age. Our anxious brain was very useful to us—families that had someone who worried more than other people would have been safer. They would have stayed away from water supplies that sickened people when they last visited that spot, and would have been mistrustful of strangers.

Notice that our brains were able to adapt to many different conditions, partly because what we did changed the way our brains worked. This is very important—if a person flees from an anxiety-provoking situation, the brain learns it is dangerous and is more anxious the next time that situation comes up. If a person stays in an anxiety-provoking situation, the brain learns it can tolerate that situation. Notice that we do not say that the brain will stop being anxious in a situation. Anxiety usually does go down when we stay in an anxiety-generating situation, but even if it doesn't, we are rewiring our brain to show ourselves we can handle it. Increasing anxiety tolerance is the goal of CBT for anxiety and OCD.

AVOIDANCE AND SAFETY BEHAVIORS

What situations are your anxious clients avoiding? What safety behaviors are they using? Avoidance and safety behaviors both work to reduce anxiety in the short run, so they feel like they are useful. However, they reinforce to the amygdala, the fear and emotion processing center of the brain, that the situation is too hard or dangerous. Avoidance and safety behaviors can be actual behaviors, but they also can be thoughts and very subtle. Anything that reassures is a safety behavior.

LIST OF COMMON SAFETY BEHAVIORS

- Needing to have a water bottle
- Being with a safe person (parent, teacher, spouse)
- Staying close to home
- Checking pulse
- Always having a throw-up bag
- Reassurance seeking
- Distracting from anxiety-generating thoughts
- Avoiding eye contact/wearing sunglasses
- Being nice/avoiding conflict
- Carrying a cell phone

BRAIN EDUCATION

Clients with anxiety are understandably afraid of the way their brains have been working. Educating each client that anxiety and OCD are false alarms, that the feelings and thoughts are distressing but not dangerous, is crucial to helping prepare them for exposure. On the next page is a simple picture of the brain that you can give to your clients to help understand what is going on.

HERE'S HOW TO TELL THE STORY TO YOUR CLIENTS

We always start by drawing a human brain, which sounds difficult but is easy when you know how. Begin by drawing a simple thought bubble, really an oval with a point on the bottom right. Then follow the script on page 38. If you really don't want to draw or don't want your clients to draw, you can copy the one on the next page. However, most of us learn better by doing things, and it is very satisfying for most people to draw a brain. Kids especially enjoy showing their parents what they learned, and it is quite fun to watch how amazed the parents are to have their child show them a brain they drew! The following two pages demonstrate for your clients how to draw the brain, and how to explain anxiety in the brain.

Human Brain

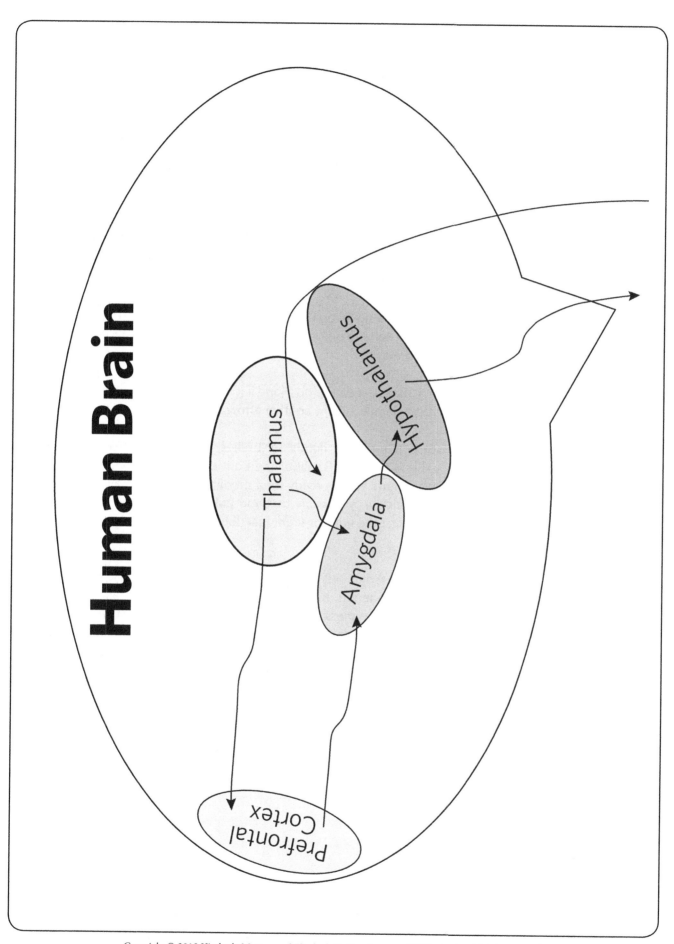

Thalamus

Hypothalamus

Amygdala

Prefrontal Cortex

Script for Brain Education

Starting with the thought bubble, add the four brain structures pictured, with the prefrontal cortex in the front of the brain and the amygdala, thalamus, and hypothalamus close together in the center.

"The prefrontal cortex is where we think things through, where we attribute meaning to things. It is what makes us human." (Put your hand on your forehead to show where this is.) "It is not where the problem with the anxious brain starts." (Draw an arrow up from the spinal column to the thalamus.)

"Everything we feel in our body travels as a signal up the spinal cord to the thalamus. The thalamus is a newness detector. It asks 'Is it new?' It sends a quick message to the amygdala and a more distant message to the cortex." (Draw those arrows.)

"The amygdala is a danger monitor. It asks, 'Is it dangerous?' and if it is new and might be dangerous, it sends a quick message to the hypothalamus." (Draw another arrow.)

"The hypothalamus begins a cascade that quickly floods our bodies with adrenalin." (Draw arrow back down the spinal column.) "This is the WHOOSH!!! of the fight-or-flight reaction. Our hearts race, our palms sweat, our stomachs churn. We are ready for a predator. If you have ever touched something hot…" (touch your desk quickly) "you know that you pull your hand back before you can even say the word *hot*. That's how fast the fight-or-flight reaction goes off." (Snap your fingers). "Just like that."

"But meanwhile, the prefrontal cortex has information." (Draw one last arrow.) "It may say it's dangerous or it may say it isn't dangerous, but the fight-or-flight reaction has already gone off. So now up the spinal column comes the message that your heart is beating fast, your palms are sweating, and your stomach is churning. Look, it hits the thalamus again, and guess what it's going to say to the amygdala. Notice how this has now become a reaction to the reaction, and usually now the cortex is saying, 'Oh no, I feel all these terrible feelings, something bad must be happening to me!'"

BRAIN EDUCATION

The script on page 38 is a teaching example. We tailor the words to the cognitive and educational level of the person we are talking to, but it does not need to be any more complicated than this. It takes just a few minutes in our session, and yet it gives us a whole new way to communicate about these powerful, unpleasant feelings.

Crucial to explaining the anxious brain is recognizing that anxiety disorders are not fear reactions that are helpful. Elizabeth felt helpful fear last year when a deer ran in front of her car while she was driving home at 60 miles an hour, and once when she was picking blackberries and a snake looking for mice slithered past her foot. She was very grateful for her fight-or-flight reaction in those moments as it helped her to swerve and yet maintain control over her car, and carefully but quickly move out of the prickly blackberry patch until the snake had gone away.

In anxiety disorders, fight or flight is a false alarm. Your brain can either provide completely false information, as it may do with OCD, or it can exaggerate discomfort, as it does with GAD. Helping a client understand that their brain can be glitchy and give them bad information is a crucial step to helping them get well.

THE ROLE OF AVOIDANCE
IN MAINTAINING ANXIETY DISORDERS

What is your first instinct when you come across something that feels uncomfortable? Do you avoid it? Try to reframe it so it doesn't feel so uncomfortable? Ask others if they feel as uncomfortable as you do? Seek reassurance to do the thing that is going to create discomfort? Any or all of these are normal responses to stressful triggers.

Kimberly was reminded of this when she was scheduled to fly to New York City to give a workshop in the middle of January. As it got closer and people in Erie, Pennsylvania, were talking about the snowstorm heading their way, she started to feel anxious. She began to wonder why she had agreed to give a workshop in the middle of winter. She thought about driving instead of flying. She started asking people—just about anyone who would listen—if they thought it was crazy to fly in a snowstorm to New York. She just wanted out of the entire travel and its potential to be stressful and anxiety-provoking.

This avoidance behavior is a key piece to the maintenance of anxiety disorders. Engaging in safety behaviors like avoidance is linked to a perceived threat. If we never engage in the actual experience creating our fear, we never give our brain a chance to disconfirm this threat. As a result, our brain learns that there must have been a danger that you narrowly avoided, which leads to your amygdala sending out more danger signals the next time you experience something similar.

Let's look at this with Kimberly's example. If she were to drive instead of fly or cancel her trip to New York, her brain would have learned that flying in bad weather is dangerous. It might even decide to add on that flying to New York is dangerous. And if it really wanted to take advantage of her vulnerability, it would decide that flying in general is dangerous.

This is how, through avoidance, anxiety is formed and maintained.

YOUR TURN

What is something that has recently triggered your fears or anxiety?

_____

_____

_____

What did you do about it?

_____

_____

_____

_____

Whom did you engage for support and what did you say?

_____

_____

_____

_____

Did you end up engaging in the experience that made you fearful or anxious?

_____

_____

_____

_____

Before learning these new concepts, most people with anxiety will avoid things that cause them anxiety. It's natural. Avoidance feels like it works, because anxiety levels usually fall, but it causes tremendous suffering and missing all kinds of situations that would be important for a rich, full life. Additionally, avoidance does not help us move forward with helping our brains cope with anxiety.

Teaching our brains involves both the cognitive (the prefrontal cortex: the front part of the brain diagram) and the behavioral (the thalamus, amygdala, and hypothalamus) areas.

The amygdala is an experiential learner. It learns not to send danger signals only by doing the things it has feared before (Gold, 2015). We call this exposure. Help your clients understand the false alarm of anxiety by asking, "Does the smoke detector ever go off in your house?" Most people will say yes, when they burn the toast or the pizza, or some other common household activity. Great. Ask, "What do you do when the pizza burns and the smoke detector goes off?" Most people will say they open the window, they fan the air below the smoke detector, or they take the battery out of the alarm. Think about the role of the smoke detector—just like the amygdala, it is designed to keep us safe, and we are glad to have it around in an emergency. However, if we burn the pizza, we know to say, "Oh well, it's just a burned pizza," and ignore the alarm. That's what we want our clients to learn to do with anxiety triggers—"Oh well, it's just anxiety."

MEDICINE FOR ANXIETY

Research shows that CBT is very effective in treating anxiety. Medicines in the family of SSRIs are about equally effective as CBT, and the two together might be slightly more effective (Van Apeldoorn et al., 2008) than either strategy on its own. Medication works by calming the fight-or-flight circuit, allowing people to do more activities they have been avoiding with less anxiety.

We often tell clients that taking medication is like using swimmies in a swimming pool. They help keep you afloat until you learn how to swim. Importantly, the effectiveness of CBT persists through time, while medication only works when someone takes it. We are happy to have clients use medicine and to have clients who do not want to use medicine. The only exception is if a client is avoiding important activities such as school (in children) or work (in adults), or suffering so greatly that they cannot begin the first steps of CBT. In that case, we recommend that they see a primary-care provider or psychiatrist to try medication in addition to CBT. Exposure and response prevention will help create new circuits/information for the brain while medication just quiets the fear response to help them participate in ERP.

Chapter Highlights

- Teach every anxious client about their anxious brain.
- The fight-or-flight reaction is normal and helpful in danger.
- Avoidance does not solve anxiety.
- The amygdala is an experiential learner.
- Refer clients for medication if they are avoiding important activities or unable to participate in ERP.
- The treatment results of CBT are long-lasting.

TAKE THE NEXT STEP

Your homework for this chapter is to tell someone else (a friend or a client) how to draw the anxious brain. How did it go?

_____

_____

_____

_____

_____

_____

Chapter 5

The Art of Exposure and Response Prevention

Exposure and response prevention (ERP), a form of cognitive behavioral therapy, is a crucial part of the evidence-based treatment for anxiety and OCD. Often, therapists engage in insight-oriented or psychodynamic therapy. The therapist might ask: "What happened in your childhood that may have led to this fear; why do you think you feel anxious?" Or they might spend a lot of time helping their client replace their anxious thoughts with more positive thoughts. However nice these approaches might feel, a primary, evidenced-based treatment that will actually create new brain circuits includes practicing exposure and response prevention with feared situations while learning to tolerate anxious feelings (Goldin et al., 2013).

In talking to the hundreds of therapists we have trained in ERP, we know how therapists new to this technique can feel anxious learning it. We remember one therapist who had been working with a boy who was afraid of bees, who told us almost tearfully, "I just couldn't bring myself to get stung by a bee on purpose. I think I failed with this client." If those feelings seem familiar to you, read on, knowing you are in good company with your fear and self-doubt. Our goal for this chapter is for you to feel confident in being able to do exposure therapy because you have tried it yourself. And, no, you don't have to get stung by a bee to be a good ERP therapist.

One of the things we do with our clients, and with clinicians who attend our workshops, is to give them a Warheads candy before we explain ERP. (These are extremely sour candies with a sweet middle that you can get in the candy section of your grocery story.) We eat the candy with them and once we have gotten to the sweet part, we discuss how eating this candy is like treating anxiety.

People usually get it pretty quickly. They often say, "You have to handle the bad to get to the good" or, "You have to tolerate the suffering to reap the rewards." Some people really have a hard time with sucking through the sour until they get to the sweet. This can be a conversation of its own and can give you some information about how powerful uncomfortable feelings are for your client. Then we continue with educating about exposure and response prevention.

Exposure is when you purposely engage in a feared situation by exposing yourself to the trigger that creates the fear and the feelings that are experienced in the feared situation.

Response prevention is when you refrain from engaging in any behavior that takes you away from the feared situation or from the emotional experience. These include avoidance, compulsions (both mental and behavioral), safety behaviors, and escape behaviors.

RIDING THE WAVE OF ANXIETY

Not only is it important to eliminate avoidance behaviors, it is equally important to tolerate the accompanying anxiety. We often call this riding the wave of anxiety. When you stay with an exposure until the anxiety decreases, you develop anxiety tolerance (Salkovskis, 1991). If you retreat from an anxiety-provoking situation before your anxiety has decreased and you have not developed the ability to handle the feelings, you have only taught your brain that the situation is indeed dangerous, and you complete the anxiety circuit, which ensures that you will feel anxiety the next time you encounter this situation/trigger.

The brain is wired to learn experientially if something is actually dangerous by seeing if we flee or stay. Flee, and you teach your brain *it is dangerous*, and get more anxiety the next time. Stay, and you teach your brain *I can tolerate it*, and build your self-confidence. Mindfulness can help teach the necessary skills to ride the wave of anxiety (Chapter 8).

During an exposure, you can use the SUDS scale to help the client stay in an exposure until their SUDS level decreases by 50%. They continue to do the same exposure, multiple times, until their beginning SUDS level is 50% of where they started.

For example, Joe had several fears he was working on in therapy. They all involved heights, which triggered his fear of dying a scary, painful death. His SUDS scale was as follows:

Rank	Trigger situation	SUDS (0-10)	What I do to feel better
1	Flying	10	Avoid
2	Hiking a mountain	8	Avoid
3	Riding a roller coaster	6	Avoid
4	Climbing a lookout tower	4	Avoid

Using our collaborative CBT model, Joe and Kimberly decided the place to start his ERP was by climbing a lookout tower. He set up a day and time to go to the lookout tower, and planned to keep climbing the tower until his anxiety levels decreased to a 2.

Joe found that the lookout tower was not as tall or as difficult as he had imagined it would be—his anxiety was never a 4, and staying at the top for 30 minutes was boring for him! Joe agreed he needed a more difficult task, but the amusement park was closed, so he could not take on his next-highest-ranked task, riding a roller coaster. He decided instead to find other high buildings to climb and look out of until his initial fear was a 2 and he could handle the accompanying fears and feelings. Joe had quickly developed the type of willingness to face his fears and curiosity about finding exposures that would lead to success, and it all started with that first exposure.

Exposure and Response Prevention Hierarchy— *Sample Topics*

An example of fear hierarchies.

GERM HIERARCHY

SUDS level	Situation
3	Using a public bathroom, putting toilet paper on the seat
3	Shaking hands with a stranger
4	Using your fingertip (and not your knuckle) when pressing buttons on an elevator
5	Shaking hands with a friend
5	Sharing a drink with a friend
5	Using the bathroom at your friend's house
5	Eating food after it has dropped on the floor in your home
7	Using a public bathroom, not putting toilet paper on the seat
8	Riding public transportation
8	Sharing a plate of food with a friend
8	Eating food after it is dropped on the floor of your friend's home
9	Eating at a salad bar
10	Being around someone who is sick with a stomach bug or cold / flu

DRIVING HIERARCHY

SUDS level	Situation
3	Driving on local suburban roads
4	Driving on two-lane highways
5	Driving on city streets
8	Driving on elevated highways
8	Driving through tunnels
9	Driving over bridges
10	Driving on major highways

YOUR TURN

Write a trigger list with SUDS scores for a client you are working with.

Trigger List			
Ranking	Trigger situation	SUDS (0–10)	What I do to feel better

THE EXPOSURE EXPERIENCE

To set your client up for a successful exposure experience, there are a few things that are helpful to remember:

- Ask them to write a letter to themselves stating what anxiety has taken from them (peace, work, healthy relationships, happiness) and why they are choosing to do ERP (what do they value, what do they want their life to look like, why?). See the sample motivational letter on the next page.

- Educate your client about the brain and why ERP along with anxiety tolerance is what will help them create healthier responses to anxiety and new brain circuitry.

- Remind them that this is a team approach. You will both be detectives, understanding how anxiety takes advantage of them at vulnerable moments and finding creative solutions to developing bravery during their exposures. Although you will work together on developing the exposure homework, your client has the last say in what they will actually be practicing.

- Explain your role as teacher, coach, trainer, cheerleader.

- Discuss the importance of learning how to expect, accept, and allow anxiety.

- Stress the importance of doing exposure and response prevention for themselves—not for you or others.

OCD Motivational Letter

OCD has taken my self-esteem, my ability to be happy, and my ability to feel comfortable around other people. I feel judged so often. OCD has taken away my ability to contribute to family's financial needs and to the greater community.

The more power I give you, OCD, the more depressed I get. I feel like I have to fight two demons and I just want to give up. I wait for support from others, but you keep me focused on how I'll never succeed and so I give up again. I feel like a failure and I'm angry so often because I feel alienated from the rest of the world. I don't know what my place is or why I'm even here.

You have taken this from me, OCD. By not working, I thought I would have more peace and I could work on getting better. Instead, it has only brought on different worries that paralyze me as well. Working or not, I can't escape the uncomfortableness and anxiety that each one brings. I feel confused. I don't know if I should keep listening to you or take a chance and see what the other side is like.

I may fail. I may disappoint my family. But I have to try because what if I succeed? I might begin to feel better about myself. I will be able to better provide for my family. I will be forced into a more structured setting which may improve my sleep. I won't have to feel guilty about spending money. I will be participating in the community and might even develop a friendship.

I know that to accomplish this, it will mean I have to forge through discomfort, anxiety, doubt, and fears of failure. However, if I don't try, I'll never know if I would have succeeded and I am certain the depression will continue, worsen, and destroy me. I *will* walk through this pain. I *will* return to work!

TYPES OF EXPOSURE AND RESPONSE PREVENTION (ERP)

This is ERP in or out of the office with your client. There are several different ways to do this, which are explained below. This helps you see their cognitive and behavioral response to the trigger and allows you to work with them to practice healthier responses. Many therapists skip this part and just give ERP as homework. In vivo exposures provide essential information to help your clients be successful at home. Don't skip this!

Spontaneous. These are exposures that happen naturally to our clients. They may be stressful situations that they are in the habit of avoiding or triggers to their anxiety disorder that happen within their day that are not planned. These can be difficult to tolerate. It is helpful to role-play them in session and have a discussion about the best way to handle spontaneous exposures.

Imaginary/script. These are done when the thing your client fears cannot be practiced. It may be something that they fear they did in the past and are obsessing over (What if I had an abortion?) or something they currently fear (I'm afraid I'll kill someone). In an imaginary script, you have your client write down their feared situation as though it is their worst nightmare with a bad ending. They can then record it on audio and play it over and over until they habituate to the thoughts and feelings, or they can read it over and over until their SUDS level decreases by 50% or they get bored with the exposure.

Interoceptive. This type of exposure is often used with panic disorder. Most people with panic attacks don't have triggers because the fear is of the panic sensations themselves. In this type of exposure, they practice inducing the symptoms of panic and changing their response to those feelings/physiological sensations. One example of this is to practice hyperventilating by breathing through straws and not using your nose to breathe. Doing this for one minute with your client will induce a variety of symptoms, including sweating, dizziness, chest pressure, and feeling like you can't get enough air. This provides for a fertile discussion on how your clients talk to themselves about these sensations, what to do when they get the feelings, and how they can teach their brains to handle them.

Planned Practice. These are exposures that you will set up, in session, with your client for them to practice several times a day in-between sessions. It is important that you and your client work together to set up exposures that will produce enough anxiety to learn new responses, but not so much anxiety that it sets them up to abandon the practice. Let your client know that this practice will not go perfectly. Some days will be better than others. Success is in the trying. When they return for their next session, you will have a lot to discuss with them about how the exposures went and what they can change to help them be more successful.

SETTING UP AN EXPOSURE

Remember our client, James, who had the sudden onset of panic disorder on the subway? Remember that his first exposure experiments were at a SUDS level of 6 because nothing was lower than that on his trigger list? He chose to work on eating small meals three times a day and going for a walk every day. He predicted he would have a SUDS rating of 6 for these activities, but he found he only had a 2 for the first two days, and after that he was at a 0 for these activities.

When he came back in for his second session, James brought his wife and asked that Elizabeth help her learn how to be his coach. James felt angry that his anxiety was keeping him from going on the subway, and he wanted to jump to the top item on his list and practice with his wife on the subway, a SUDS rating of 10. This would not normally be the next step in CBT therapy. However, we want to recognize that, for a variety of reasons, sometimes exposure will not or cannot move smoothly up the hierarchy.

Examples of starting in a different place on the hierarchy are situations like James's, when the client wants to take on a specific challenge, or with a situation like fear of flying when a trip is coming up too quickly to do all the easier steps first. As long as the client understands that they will likely have anxiety and that they must be prepared to stay in the situation until their anxiety is at 50% of what it was, it is very possible to get well quickly by choosing an approach like James's. We don't want clients to be afraid of exposure at high SUDS levels, and we don't want you to be afraid of it, either.

HOW TO HELP DURING AN EXPOSURE

When practicing in vivo exposures, there are several ways to help your client during the exposure. A mindful approach can make the difference between a successful exposure and a frustrating one. This means that your client will need to learn how to stay in the present. Having them describe their physiological sensations of anxiety and their thoughts about the experience will help you to coach them through the exposure. Asking them to describe their experience with facts, not fears, helps them begin to develop a new way of talking about an anxious experience that takes power away from the anxiety. Another mindfulness skill is to instruct them to use their senses to describe their surroundings. This can also help your client to slow down their response to the trigger.

Paying attention to their breath can be helpful, but only to help clients regulate their breath with a longer exhale. People with anxiety tend to breathe in too much oxygen, which supports the fight/flight response. Focusing on their breathing as a way to hold a space for the exposure experience while they ride out the wave of anxiety is an appropriate way to use their breath. Breathing out activates the rest and digest response and tends to counter the fight or flight response, so the longer the exhale, the better.

Celebrating any effort they put toward practicing ERP, as well as small results, will help encourage your client to stay in the exposure and outlast their anxiety. Paying attention to their courageous efforts, rather than the outcome, is also helpful.

Talk to them about changing their relationship with fear. Fear and anxiety will always be a part of their life. It's how they respond to these experiences that can change the course of their anxiety disorder.

It can also be helpful for your client to have some clarity about why they are willing to do exposure therapy. Identifying what your client values and going back to the motivational letter they wrote to themselves can be a clear reminder of why they are facing their fears. We have a client who has panic disorder with agoraphobia who hung a sign across the threshold of her family room, saying "Don't look back, you are not going that way!" This helped her practice her ERP at home by reminding her that she values a healthy future more than a small, isolated life with anxiety.

Changing the emotion during an exposure gives the power back to the client. Anger, tears, and frustration give power to anxiety. Laughter can deflate it. One word of caution: Your client needs to be on board with laughing through an exposure or seeing the ridiculous in their fears. If you make light of an exposure without your client agreeing, it could backfire, leaving your client feeling like you don't understand how powerful the anxiety feels.

USING REWARDS

Whether you are working with a child, teenager, or adult, rewards can make a big difference with exposure and response prevention. Remember, you are rewarding bravery, so it is helpful to discuss what bravery looks like. Rewards are given for trying, whether the outcome is habituation to anxiety or not. Early on, you want to make a list of things that may help motivate your client to do an exposure. I have a reward box in my office filled with items from the Dollar Store. This can be helpful for young kids. Teens appreciate verbal praise. Adults are pretty good at finding ways to reward themselves.

Small
- Earn screen time
- Frappuccino
- Sleepover with friend

Medium
- A dollar for every exposure
- Dinner out at restaurant of choice
- Movie at theater

Large
- A new tent for camping
- A dog/cat/reptile
- A weekend skiing

DEVELOPING HOMEWORK

Practicing outside of sessions is the key to overcoming an anxiety disorder or OCD. Psychoeducation includes teaching your client that, in order for their brain to develop new circuits, they have to practice a new response consistently, frequently, and intensely. This means that the more often they practice, the better.

It is also important for them to create opportunities to practice daily, trying not to skip any days. Once they have faced most of the triggers from their list, it is time for them to challenge the intensity of their exposures. Although you may wonder why it is important to do extreme exposures, research has found that it can be the best way for your client to teach their brain that they are no longer afraid (Gillihan, Williams, Malcoun, Yadin, & Foa, 2012).

Also, teach your client to start small and work up their trigger hierarchy. Starting too high can be overwhelming. Have them stay in the exposure until their SUDS level decreases by 50%, and have them do the exposure several times a day until their initial exposure SUDS is 50% lower than it was when they started. Once they have achieved this, they can move on to the next trigger in their hierarchy.

The Exposure Practice Record worksheet on the next page can be given to your client to take home and record their exposure practice. This provides accountability at home and allows them to be mindful of their thoughts, feelings, and actions before, during, and after an exposure. It also provides helpful information for you to discuss with your client in your next session. We are also providing you with an Exposure Log (page 53), which is a shorter variation of the Exposure Practice Record. You and your client can decide, together, which would be more helpful to their practice.

Example

Eleven-year-old Hannah agreed to face her fear of spiders using planned exposures. She started by writing the word *spiders*. This gave her a 3 on a scale of 0–10. She continued to write the word *spiders* in her notebooks at school and on her bathroom mirror, and even wrote a story for her English class about spiders that week. When she no longer felt anxiety about writing the word *spider*, she moved on to googling images of spiders. This gave her a 5 on her SUDS scale, so she agreed to look at pictures of spiders before she went on to social media every day. When her anxiety came down to a 2 or 3, she agreed to take a friend and look for spiders every day during recess. This gave her a SUDS of 9, but her friend was making it kind of fun, so she quickly went down to a 5. By the end of her practice, she was able to handle her anxiety during spontaneous exposures to spiders.

It is important for your client to keep a journal of their exposure practice. Without keeping a record of what they have done, the anxiety bully keeps focusing on what is still to come, not how much progress has been made. The journal should include the following:

- What the exposure was.
- SUDS levels before, during, and after the exposure.
- Their thoughts before, during, and after the exposure.
- Physical sensations they experienced during the exposure and how long those sensations lasted.

. . . .

Exposure Practice Record

Date: _____

Exposure practice: _____

Prior to exposure: anticipatory distress (0–10): _____

Thoughts, feelings, and behaviors you noticed **before the exposure**: _____

_____

_____

_____

Thoughts, feelings, and behaviors **during the exposure**: _____

_____

_____

_____

Thoughts, feelings, and behaviors **after completing the exposure**: _____

_____

_____

_____

Number of minutes you did the exposure: _____

Maximum distress during the task (0–10): _____

Distress at the end of the task (0–10): _____

Any attempts to avoid your emotions (distraction, safety behaviors, reassurance, etc.)?

_____

_____

_____

What did you take away from this exposure practice?

_____

_____

_____

Did your feared outcomes occur? If so, how were you able to cope with them?

_____

_____

_____

. . . .

Exposure Log

Date: _____

Exposure: _____

SUDS level (0–10): Before: _____ During: _____ After: _____

Thoughts: Before: _____ During: _____ After: _____

Physical sensations: _____

Duration of physical sensations:_____

Date: _____

Exposure: _____

SUDS level (0–10): Before: _____ During: _____ After: _____

Thoughts: Before: _____ During: _____ After: _____

Physical sensations: _____

Duration of physical sensations:_____

Date: _____

Exposure: _____

SUDS level (0–10): Before: _____ During: _____ After: _____

Thoughts: Before: _____ During: _____ After: _____

Physical sensations: _____

Duration of physical sensations:_____

YOUR TURN

Using this information, expose yourself to something that creates fear/anxiety for you and fill out the Exposure Practice Record.

WORKING WITH RESISTANCE TO EXPOSURE

What if your client refuses to do an exposure? Try not to let anxiety bully you. A good coach understands how powerful anticipatory anxiety can feel for someone starting an exposure. A helpful response when they resist would be, "You may not believe you can do the exposure we planned. What part of it can you do?" Then you become a team again, trying to find some small part of the exposure that they can practice. It doesn't matter how small the exposure is—once they have success, it will be easier to take on the next part of their exposure and tolerate more anxiety. Resistance is normal. Remember, it is our instinct to listen to our amygdala and to avoid discomfort and danger. Here are a few tips on how to handle resistance:

- Don't ask, "Do you want to do this exposure?" A client will never say they want to. Would you want to do something that terrifies you? Instead, explain the rationale behind doing exposures and give them a choice of what level of exposure to begin with.

- If they say they don't have time to practice exposures, ask them how much time they spend engaging in avoidance or compulsive behaviors. Help them come up with a way to get around these perceived obstacles, including using cognitive restructuring.

- Return to psychoeducation. Ask them to teach you about their brain and why exposure therapy is helpful.

- Break the ERP into smaller parts. Often we start too high on the hierarchy. Just take responsibility for making a mistake and starting them too high. Then see what they can do, instead of talking about what they can't do.

- Accountability is very helpful with resistance. Remember to bring in family members and friends to boost the energy around the therapy, and bring in some accountability to practice daily. Text messaging a friend when an exposure is complete can really be helpful.

- Sometimes people don't have support systems to keep them accountable. In these cases, we each have the client leave us a voicemail or email us at the end of the day to tell us they completed their exposures. Ask them to keep a detailed journal so you can discuss their experience at your next session.

WHAT NOT TO DO

Kimberly recently had a client who had OCD around hyper-responsibility. She had been triggered by her son's back hurting. She took him to the doctor and told the doctor that she had been cracking his back. She was told to have him get physical therapy. In the session, she wanted to know if she had done the right thing by telling the doctor that she had cracked his back. Kimberly told her she didn't think it really mattered. Many people crack their backs. She then wanted to know if she should tell the physical therapist about the back cracking. She also told Kimberly she was never again going to crack his back and asked what Kimberly thought about back cracking.

This is an example of "co-compulsing." Kimberly got caught in her compulsion to be a responsible person by answering her questions and participating in the conversation about back cracking. Many therapists co-compulse without realizing that they are giving more power to the client's anxiety by engaging the content of their fear.

Here are some things *not* to do when engaging in exposure and response prevention:

- Do not connect to the content of the fear. Instead, identify it as anxiety and help them to live with the uncertainty and distress of not knowing the answer.

- Do not reassure a client. Any reassurance you give to make them feel better during an exposure connects the circuit in their brain that tells their amygdala that they can't handle the thought/feeling because you had to help them feel better.

- Do not engage in psychodynamic processing. It is a rabbit hole you don't want to go down. Understanding where the fears come from will not help them change their brain—practicing ERP can help change their brain.

- Do not teach them relaxation. Our goal is to help the client handle the feeling, and relaxation tries to get rid of the feeling. Relaxation can be helpful as a part of a wellness plan to help someone stay under their stress threshold. It is not helpful during an exposure, when a client needs to learn to ride the wave of anxiety.

- Do not listen to their anxiety story for any length of time. Be respectful and socialize the client to tell you the highlights of their trigger, but explain that telling the story can be a part of a compulsion they use to feel better. It is okay to politely interrupt your client when they are engaged in storytelling, explaining what you need from the story and moving on to set up ERP practice with the fear.

WORKING BRAVELY

Talking to the therapist who was working with the boy who was afraid of bees, we learned that she and the boy had made tremendous progress. They had told a story about bees, watched videos about bees, and made small paper finger puppets and buzzed them around the office. His mother had learned to coach him through exposures at home as well, and the boy was able to go back to his summer camp, which he had been avoiding because they ate lunch outside and he was afraid that would attract bees. This was a tremendous success, especially because the therapist had no previous training in CBT. The therapist was pleased when we pointed out her success! Sometimes we do have to do extreme exposure, and we will talk about that in Chapter 10, but that was not needed in this and many other cases. Make sure to give yourself credit for the steps you are taking to learn ERP and teach these important skills to your client. Therapy is not like Einstein's field equations that explain the effects of gravity on space-time, where complicated and fixed rules apply. ERP is flexible. No two therapists and clients will approach the same type of problem in the same way. No two exposures will go the exact same way.

If you can, get case consultation with another therapist who is doing this work, because anxiety will trip you up whether you are a new or experienced therapist. That's part of the process of treating anxiety and OCD, so learn from the experience and get back to doing the important work of treating clients who need your help.

Chapter Highlights

- Exposure and response prevention (ERP) is the primary evidence-based treatment for anxiety and OCD.

- Avoidance plays a major role in maintaining anxiety disorders.

- It is important to develop the ability to ride the wave of anxiety when doing ERP.

- There are several types of exposure practice that can be helpful in and outside the office, depending on the type of anxiety.

- Preparing a client for exposure will help them to be successful.

- You are a team. Doing exposures together will help you both get clarity about the fear and the thoughts and feelings that accompany the fear. This will help you develop the best exposures for the client to practice at home.

- Rewarding a client after exposure will help motivate them.

- Starting small with ERP is the best way to experience success and develop the ability to do more challenging exposures.

- Have fun with practice. Changing the emotion from angst to laughter can deflate anxiety.
- Involve family members and friends to be a part of the solution and help with accountability.
- The only way to change an experience with a fear is to practice facing it, feeling it, and doing the opposite many times.

TAKE THE NEXT STEP

Develop homework for a client of yours. (Remember to be specific about what they will be doing)

_____

_____

_____

_____

How often should your client practice this?

_____

_____

How long should your client practice the exposure?

_____

_____

What safety behaviors/compulsions should your client refrain from?

_____

_____

_____

_____

Write an example of how your client could talk themselves through the exposure.

_____

_____

_____

Chapter 6

Involving Family Members and Friends in Treatment

From the first session, we ask clients to bring their family members and friends to a session so we can learn more about the client's anxiety, and their family and friends can learn more about how to be a part of the recovery process. Family members can be an important part of the assessment process, giving you a better understanding of the role they play in accommodating anxiety. As discussed in Chapter 3, it is important to understand both the symptoms the client is experiencing and what they and others do in response to those symptoms. Equally important is the ability for family/friends to learn about anxiety, how to respond when their loved one is triggered, and how to coach them through an exposure.

Recently, Kimberly was evaluating a woman who worried about bad things happening to her children, who are now teenagers and young adults. Her response to her fears over the years was to become hyperaware of potential danger for her children. She also prevented them from going places and doing things that might be unsafe. Kimberly asked her to invite her husband and children to a session. She was willing to have her husband come in, but initially refused to involve her children in order to "protect" them from her illness. Involving family members is often like doing an exposure.

As with any exposure work, Kimberly agreed to start with her husband. He was extremely helpful in that he was gentle with her, but he was clear with Kimberly about how her anxiety had affected every member of the family. They all adored her, but he no longer knew what to do to calm her fears. He reassured her almost constantly. Kimberly taught him about anxiety and the brain. She also reviewed what he can say and do that will be helpful and what is not helpful. They were both grateful to understand her anxiety better and left feeling hopeful that there is good treatment.

At the end of the session, her husband told her that he really wanted their children to attend a session. He was concerned about their 20-year-old daughter, who was showing symptoms of OCD. This triggered the client's worry, believing that she did not protect her daughter from developing mental illness. They decided to wait on bringing her children in and got started with Exposure and Response Prevention (ERP). As she started to benefit from her therapy, she agreed to include her three children. They were forthright about how much they loved their mother, but how frustrating it was to grow up with anxiety parenting them. This had led to a lot of conflict between the mother and her daughter. There was a lot to teach this family about how to help their mom/wife and how to stand up to anxiety.

YOUR TURN

1. Do you involve family members when you treat a client with anxiety or OCD?

2. What do you do when a client resists bringing family into therapy?

_____

_____

_____

3. Have you had a client not have any supports? What do you do then?

_____

_____

_____

4. Describe a time when bringing family/friends made a difference in the treatment outcome for a client:

_____

_____

_____

_____

_____

_____

ASSESSMENT OF FAMILY ACCOMMODATION

Initially, it is important to assess the role family and friends play in accommodation. Remember from Chapter 4: Anything the family/friend does to help your client feel better is only connecting the anxiety circuit and ensuring future anxiety. After joining with the client and their loved ones and teaching them about the anxious brain, we ask several questions: What do you do when Tom's anxiety gets triggered? How is or isn't it helpful? Have you found yourself reassuring Tom when he asks for it? Do you participate in any of his compulsions? Do you wait for him to complete his routines before you leave the house? Do you help Tom to avoid things or situations that make him anxious? Do you help him so that he can complete his compulsions? Is there anything that you don't do because of Tom's anxiety, including leisure activities? In an effort to bring some humor into our session, we often warn: "Whatever you tell me can and will be used against you during an ERP session," and we laugh.

During your assessment, it may be helpful for you to have the family members fill out the Family Accommodation Scale for OCD (Lebowitz et al., 2012). As you gather this information, you are able to get a clearer picture of whom anxiety goes to for help. We tell families that anxiety will always go to the weakest link, so we need to make sure everyone involved is strong! The way they get strong is by having good information, which will come from you.

You will also be gathering information about compulsions and safety behaviors that must be addressed for your client to recover fully. Often, the client does not even see these behaviors as a part of their anxiety disorder because they have just become a part of the way they live their life. If they don't see it, how can they share it with you? This is why involving family and friends is so crucial.

EDUCATING FAMILY AND FRIENDS

After assessing for accommodation, we begin to teach the family about the anxious brain (see Chapter 4). Part of what we explain is why it is so frustrating to talk with someone who is in an anxious state. Because their loved one is being driven by fight/flight chemicals, they are not in their wise mind.

So instead of talking to Tom, from the previous example, they are actually talking to anxiety, who is a formidable opponent. During this session, we often ask the client to draw a picture of their anxious brain (Chapter 4) and explain it to their family/friend. End with asking how they will know that their loved one is better. What will be different in their lives? What will they do that they haven't for a while? What will things be like at home when this is better?

YOUR TURN

Create a script of what you might say to teach a family member about anxiety.

_____

_____

_____

_____

_____

_____

_____

_____

_____

_____

_____

COACHING THROUGH AN ANXIETY TRIGGER/ERP HOMEWORK

Once everyone is on the same page, we begin to teach them about how to respond in a helpful way during an anxious time or when the client is practicing their ERP homework. Role-playing, in session, can be very helpful to both the client and their family or friend. It can be very challenging to coach someone in a healthy way through anxiety, as it is often the opposite of what comes naturally. When we think we are being kind and helpful to a family member, we may actually be accommodating the anxiety.

Finally, we provide them with the following Tips for Anxiety and OCD Coaches handout and we begin to go over what these steps would actually look like when they are out of the office and practicing at home.

Be sure to have the family/friend practice coaching in session. It can be fun to have the client give their family member feedback on how they did. It can be more difficult for a family member or friend to change their language when dealing with the anxious person than for your client to practice their exposures!

Tips for Anxiety and OCD Coaches

1. Do not reassure someone who is anxious or has OCD. Validate their uncomfortable feelings and help them to tolerate them without solving the problem.

2. Remember that panic and anxiety are normal bodily reactions and are not harmful.

3. Be a cheerleader! Convince them that they can tolerate the anxiety feelings or OCD thoughts without doing anything to feel better. You know and they will learn that the anxiety will eventually decrease.

4. Challenge them to feel worse. If they can look at a spider, can they also touch the spider?

5. Help them to change the emotion: anger, frustration, and resistance all give anxiety power. Laughter can deflate it!

6. Teach your anxious person to rate their anxiety level from 0–10 (10 is a panic attack, and 0 is a breeze).

7. Have your anxious person stay with this feeling until their anxiety decreases by 50%, then challenge them to feel worse and tolerate it some more.

8. Do not be an enabler or allow the anxiety to rope you in with whatever the trigger topic is for your anxious person. Say, "I know this is the anxiety (or OCD) talking, not you."

9. Expect and allow the anxiety or OCD to reappear. The goal is not to get rid of anxious feelings— it is to live a good life and accept that anxiety will come and go.

10. Reward their hard work! (Use small gifts for young children and lots of verbal praise for older children; get creative with adults.)

Kimberly recently worked with a 7-year-old boy with severe OCD due to pediatric acute-onset neuropsychiatric syndrome (PANS). She had taught his parents and his sister how to coach him through his exposures. It took several attempts to help his mother be successful because she often tried to cajole him to do an exposure with a "sing-songy" voice. He would politely say to his mom, "No thank you, Mommy. I don't want to do that." He then would walk away. Kimberly had to model for her using clear, directive language. She could not ask him if he wanted to do the exposure, and she had to make sure she had a good reward waiting for him.

Then Kimberly worked with the dad. He was much less forgiving and resorted to being angry as soon as the boy resisted doing the exposure. Kimberly talked to him about being sure to validate how awful this feels to his son and how proud he is of him for facing his fears even though it feels bad. Kimberly encouraged the dad to share examples from his day when he struggled with his feelings/fears, and how he was able to do what he needed to do anyway.

Kimberly also taught them some ways to have fun with OCD (see Chapter 9). It turned out that the boy's 9-year-old sister was the best coach! So we developed a competition that looked like this: Dad will coach him in the morning. Sister will coach him after school. Mom will coach him after dinner. Whoever gets him to do the most exposures or the most difficult exposures wins and gets to eat a dessert with the boy that night. Everybody was excited to try this—even the young boy, because it meant he got to have dessert every night!

Chapter Highlights

- Involving family members is an important part of treating anxiety and OCD. If your client resists, treat the resistance as an exposure and don't give in to anxiety. Find one small step they are willing to take to involve family and friends.
- Identify how family and friends accommodate anxiety to get a clearer picture of rituals and safety behaviors.
- Educate family/friends about the anxious brain and how they can become part of the solution.
- Practice coaching through anxious triggers using the "Tips" handout.

TAKE THE NEXT STEP

Give an example of a time someone you care about was avoiding doing something because of anxiety.

_____

_____

_____

_____

Using the information from this chapter, how might you have coached this person to do the thing they were avoiding?

_____

_____

_____

Chapter 7

Cognitive Therapy

Cognitive therapy is a broad category of therapeutic strategies aimed at changing the way clients think about thinking. Most people are not used to thinking about the way they think, and learning that thoughts are not facts can make a tremendous difference in both mental health and overall functioning.

However, research shows that for most clients with anxiety and OCD, the behavioral treatment of exposure and response prevention (ERP) is the primary way they will get better (McManus, Van Doorn, & Yiend, 2012). Specific diagnoses, like social anxiety disorder, have been found to be more effectively treated with a cognitive component than with exposure alone, because the thoughts of most socially anxious people are quite distorted. Once clients are practicing daily exposures, and their family members are educated to be coaches, you should return to more specific cognitive work.

We say "return," because much of the psychoeducation that you did at the beginning of your work with a client is cognitive. When you asked the client to be a detective, you helped move their thoughts in a new direction from the rigid pattern they had been in before. When you suggested the client write a letter of motivation before beginning exposure, you gave them the chance to engage their cortex in helping to rewire the way the brain responds to the amygdala.

Above all, there is a cognitive component in recognizing with our clients that we must tolerate uncertainty and uncomfortable feelings. Cognitive restructuring leads to recognizing that our thoughts, actions, and feelings are all interconnected. To change our feelings, we need to change our thoughts and actions. Cognitive behavioral therapy is called just that because the cognitive and the behavioral are interwoven in treatment (Weck et al., 2015).

COGNITIVE STRATEGIES

- Automatic thoughts
- Cognitive distortions
- Bossing back
- Just a thought
- Anticipatory anxiety

- Bring it on
- Thought/action/feeling
- Thought log
- Values clarification
- Underlying assumptions/core beliefs

AUTOMATIC THOUGHTS

Automatic thoughts run like a narration through our days. For most people with anxiety and OCD, the narration is worried and negative. We are all used to our thoughts—that's why they are called automatic thoughts. However, the first step to making a change is to recognize these automatic thoughts. Stop right now, and see if you can catch any thoughts. Ask yourself, "What was I just thinking?"

YOUR TURN

What automatic thoughts do you notice right now?

_____

_____

_____

Perhaps you found yourself thinking, "Not another exercise! I just want Kimberly and Elizabeth to tell me how to do this, not to have to stop and write something down." This thought accurately reflects your feeling of frustration that you want to move on and learn how to do cognitive restructuring to help your clients, and not consider your own thoughts. Implied in this thought is that taking time to write something down is slowing down your ability to learn the technique. We can add this to the thought, then: "This is taking longer than it needs to." Your thought, of course, may be quite different from this.

Now we need to consider if the thought is actually true. Most thoughts have some subjectivity or relativism to them. The thought "I have blue eyes" is true, but it's not the way we are thinking most of the time. We might think, "My eyes look tired today" or "I'll probably need glasses when I'm older." Notice how the first thought about having blue eyes is the only one that has a truth to it. The other thoughts have either a judgment or a guess about the future that is not strictly true. I don't know if others see my eyes as looking tired or if I will need glasses when I'm older—I am just guessing at those things, and our guesses have a tendency toward the negative.

Our brains have a negative bias, which means that when two thoughts or events have relatively similar importance, we will attend more to the negative than the purely neutral or positive. Notice that our minds don't tell us that we have a negative bias or that we are guessing about the future: Our minds make us feel like our thoughts are the truth.

Catching your thoughts is tricky. To be successful teaching cognitive restructuring to your client, it is important for you to be able to do it for yourself first.

YOUR TURN

Fill out the left-hand side of the following chart with your automatic thoughts about a particular situation or event. Leave the right-hand column blank for now. If you think you are done, ask yourself, "Is there more?"

Automatic Thoughts

Situation or event: _____

Automatic Anxious/Negative Thought		Rational/Neutral Response

We like using a two-column chart for our own thoughts and with clients. The chart can be used with a middle column, however, which is where the automatic anxious/negative thought is categorized by the type of cognitive distortion that causes it.

COGNITIVE DISTORTIONS

Cognitive distortions were first described by Aaron Beck, MD, who is considered the father of cognitive therapy. Later, David Burns, MD, modified the names and provided examples of distortions.

Most of us aren't used to thinking about our thoughts. We just think. Everyone, though, has had the experience of doing something like going to a movie with a friend and talking about it afterwards, feeling as if we saw different movies. As the movie starts, you might think: "This is one of my favorite actors. I'm so glad I'm here today with my friend." Your friend is thinking: "I didn't want to see a movie today. It's so beautiful outside; I wish we had gone for a hike instead." Those different thoughts colored the perspectives and lead to different emotions about the movie. You feel happy and satisfied, while your friend feels annoyed and dissatisfied.

Our thoughts have a tremendous impact on our emotions and our experiences in life. Thoughts don't have the power to change events—neither you nor I can think the rain away—but they do have the power to shape our experience of the event. Instead of being disappointed by a rainy day, we could think, "Rain is good for growing things" or "I'm enjoying the smell of the wet pavement" (Schreiber et al., 2015).

On the next page is a list of cognitive distortions. Hand them out to your clients when you teach them cognitive restructuring. For most people, looking at this list has a tremendous ring of familiarity—"Oh, this is the type of messed-up thinking I have all the time!"

. . . .
Cognitive Distortions

1. **All-or-nothing thinking**: You don't see middle ground. You assume that if you don't get the promotion, the company wants to ease you out the door.

2. **Overgeneralization**: You extrapolate your future based on a single event. You figure that if you failed the bar exam on the first try, you're just not cut out to be a lawyer.

3. **Minimizing and maximizing**: You discount your accomplishments and inflate your errors. You made two typos in your presentation and tell yourself you've blown the whole assignment.

4. **Fortune-telling**: You predict that things will turn out badly, no matter what you say or do. Your new boyfriend does not call you as promised before a business trip, and you spend the week convinced he's breaking up with you.

5. **Emotional reasoning**: You believe how you feel is the way things are. You spill food on yourself at a restaurant and feel like a jerk, so you assume other people see you that way, too.

6. **Shoulds and oughts**: You focus on your own or other people's expectations of you. You feel you ought to help a coworker with his project—even though it will make you fall behind in your work.

7. **Tunnel vision**: You only focus on the negative aspects of a situation. "My son's teacher can't do anything right. He's insensitive and lousy at teaching."

8. **Catastrophizing**: You predict the future negatively without considering other possible outcomes.

YOUR TURN

Which of the cognitive distortions do you find familiar to your thinking?

_____

_____

_____

Now go back to your two-column list, and, knowing that your thoughts are not completely true, come up with possible alternative ways of looking at these same topics that are more rational or neutral, and write them in the right-hand column. You don't have to completely believe the new thought, but it's important that you don't completely disbelieve it, either. Notice how the goal is not to be super happy or enthusiastic; work on finding those rational and neutral thoughts and attend to them.

Automatic Thought	Rational Response
Not another exercise! I don't want to write more.	Doing this helps me recognize my own distorted thoughts and will help me teach my clients how to do this.
This is taking longer than it needs to.	I can skip it if I want, but my goal is to learn how to do this, so I will take the time to practice this technique.

EXTERNALIZING/BOSSING BACK

Anxiety and OCD produce negative automatic thoughts that feel very real. It's a trick of an overactive amygdala, as you saw in Chapter 4. Externalizing the problem by imagining the negative thoughts and the amygdala that produces them as a force apart from ourselves is another helpful cognitive strategy.

Have your client picture the part of the brain that is tricking them as a dragon, a demon, or another negative creature or image. Try out a new way of looking at these thoughts—"It's not me, it's the dragon scaring me." This creature or image is a bully. It thrives on your fear, and knows the more you avoid it and don't like it, the stronger it becomes. Try using a picture of the creature or a stuffed animal, and help your client learn to talk back to it.

Elizabeth suggests that clients try using the image of the dragon, and she has a large collection of dragons in her office to use for this work. She sets a dragon on another chair and role-plays back and forth with her client what the dragon says—"You are going to fail," "You have tried this before and it never works," "Just give up and avoid working on this" are all common dragon statements—and then works on brave things to say to the bully: "You can make me feel yucky, but I'm going to do it anyway. It's my choice to do something or not—not yours, dragon. I might have struggled with you for a long time, but I'm glad to be learning not to listen to you."

JUST A THOUGHT

Quick! Don't think about a pink elephant for the next 60 seconds! This is a great way to introduce the "just-a-thought" idea to your clients. Set a timer for 60 seconds and see if you and they can't not think of that pink elephant. Every time one of you thinks of the pink elephant, reset the timer. It's just 60 seconds, but no one can do it.

It's funny about thoughts—you can't _not_ think about something, because by definition you are thinking about it by trying not to think about it. I love this example because it makes so much sense, and because the ridiculous image of a pink elephant isn't even something that has a high emotional charge like the anxious or obsessive thoughts our clients struggle to push away. We know that the unwanted, emotional charge of thoughts is part of what gives them power.

A great cognitive strategy is to work on saying, "It's just a thought." A client's feeling that they might be a pedophile? It's just a thought. Fearing that the noise in the night is an intruder ready to kill their family? It's just a thought. Just like a pink elephant isn't real—it's just a thought—so too can identifying the fear topics as mere thoughts help allow the brain to move on to other topics instead of being stuck on the content of the fear.

ANTICIPATORY ANXIETY

You have probably noticed with your clients as they do ERP and keep records like those in Chapter 5 that the worst anxiety is usually the anticipation of a triggering event. A client with social anxiety will be at the highest SUDS level before a holiday party, and fall to a lower level during the party itself.

Retraining the brain means going through these high levels of anxiety in order to teach ourselves that we can tolerate it. Make sure to recognize with your clients the role of anticipatory anxiety—how the surge in anxiety is creating avoidance and causing more suffering in their lives. The cognitive restructuring comes from recognizing that it's difficult to get into a cool swimming pool when we are warm—we can inch in, or we can jump. Once we are in, the water is fine, but if we avoid the swimming pool because we don't want that moment of feeling cold, we miss a lot of fun in our lives.

BRING IT ON

Cognitive therapy is all about changing the way you think. A paradoxical approach uses anxiety as an opportunity for more ERP. This is a great cognitive restructuring strategy. Anxiety and OCD thrive when our clients avoid their triggers, so if they want to get well, help them see that they want to find opportunities that generate anxiety. Look for opportunities to bring on more anxiety. "I hope I feel anxious going to the mall! It will be a great opportunity to practice tolerating these feelings and shopping anyway!"

A great way to help your clients argue for and against a thought before looking for a rational thought is by completing a Thought Record.

Thought Record is a fundamental tool in cognitive behavioral therapy. It can be used to identify negative automatic thoughts and help clients see the connection between thoughts and emotions. Mary met a friend at a coffee shop. Her friend was late. Her automatic thoughts were, "She must have forgotten. Maybe she didn't really want to have coffee with me." Her anxiety level was a 5. Supporting evidence included that her friend had been late before. Contradicting evidence is that her friend initiated the coffee date and has eventually shown for previous dates. Her rational thought was, "She has been late before. I often feel anxious when people are late. That doesn't mean she does not want to have coffee with me. I can practice patience and flexibility while I wait." Mary's anxiety level after challenging her automatic negative thoughts was a 3.

Thought Record

Automatic Thought	Anxiety 0–10	Supporting Evidence	Contradicting Evidence	Rational Thought	Anxiety 0–10

VALUES CLARIFICATION

Anxiety and OCD get in the way of things that our clients value, but most people are not aware of that reality unless you point out the discrepancy between what they are doing or spending time on and what they value. Kimberly had a client who wanted to become a doctor, but he spent hours in the bathroom doing compulsions, which prevented him from studying for the boards. Once he clarified that he wanted to be a doctor more than he wanted to be alone with OCD, he had a renewed energy for tackling his obsessions and compulsions in the bathroom.

Values clarification is especially important for young adults and people with social anxiety. They may be very far from where they want to be in life due to problems with anxiety. When you bring up the topic of values clarification as you set the agenda in a therapy session with a client, some people will be glad to focus on this topic, and others will say they have no idea and it's too hard. If it is too hard for a client, back up a step. Go back to what their assumptions are about what you are going to do with values clarification. This can be a rewarding cognitive restructuring exercise.

YOUR TURN

What are your values?

_____

_____

_____

_____

What gets in the way of spending time doing what you value?

_____

_____

_____

_____

What I Value

This list offers you a chance to consider your values. There are no right or wrong answers. Circle the topics that are important to you, and add other topics to the lines below. For example, you might add something specific like "owning my own home," "traveling by airplane to visit my sister," or "having a child."

- Friendship

- Money

- Family

- Adventure

- Independence

- Being respected in my field

- Power

- Social justice

- Creativity and the arts

- Being a good person

- Helping others

- Security

_____

_____

_____

_____

_____

_____

Another great exercise is to have your clients imagine themselves 10 years from now living an ideal life, and together make a collage on a poster board with pictures that fit what that life would look like. Your goal with all of this is to make sure the client connects how anxiety and OCD are standing in the way of what they really value. This can be a great incentive to take difficult steps with exposure.

UNDERLYING ASSUMPTIONS AND CORE BELIEFS

Sometimes clients have assumptions or core beliefs that underlie their thoughts and actions. These core beliefs are often not articulated by the client because they seem so self-evident or because they feel so shameful. They are usually patterns of thought that trace back to childhood or adolescence, and arise from combinations of childhood experiences and temperament.

Core beliefs usually seem true to the client. They will take much more work than simple cognitive restructuring exercises, so if you find yourself stuck with your client on a particular topic, you may have come across a core belief. Knowing that these deeply felt beliefs have a name is important for clients, but is just a first step in the work needed to confront the power that core belief has in a person's life (Wilhelm et al., 2015).

Core Belief Chart

Belief	Typical Thought
Defectiveness/worthless	"I'm not good enough" "I'm a bad person" "I'm worthless"
Unlovable	"I'm alone" "I don't fit in" "I'm always rejected"
Abandonment	"People I love will leave me" "My partner is not interested in me"
Helpless/dependent	"I'm weak" "I'm vulnerable" "I'm needy"
Entitlement/high standards	"I'm superior" "If I don't succeed, I'm worthless/a failure"
Self-sacrifice	"I'm responsible for everyone" "My needs are unimportant" "I'm only valuable as a person if I'm helping others"
Mistrust	"If I trust people, they may hurt me"

Help your clients change core beliefs by considering the "rules" they follow due to their core beliefs. A client with high standards or perfectionism may be focused on doing everything at work perfectly. The rule they have is if it's not done perfectly, it isn't done. However, this often backfires by causing work to take too long. It can also cause difficulty working with others because the work is over-controlled, or they may come across as braggy or putting others' work down.

These problems can be serious in the workplace. Try a paradoxical exposure to test the belief. This might include asking a coworker for help or turning something in before it is done perfectly. This can feel like a tremendous risk, so consider the possible outcomes and pick something with a lower potential for risk to begin with. Even an imagination exposure or role-play with you can begin to get your client to think in a less rigid way and can be a place to start.

Another way to change is to begin to incorporate a new belief that is contrary to the core belief. Remember that we can't not think of a thought. Even something simple like pink elephants appear if we try not to think of them. However, adding a new thought can be powerful. Instead of "My work is always perfect," try "My work is good enough." Then have the client keep a record in their journal of evidence that this new belief is true. When the client turns in a report at work even though it is not perfect, have them write it in the journal. Importantly, ask them to note what happened next. What were the consequences? Your client has already seen the consequences of perfectionism. Entitlement was not what they wanted. This is a chance to try doing things differently.

Example

Here's an example of how the cognitive can be pulled together with the behavioral in therapy. Elizabeth worked with a 10-year-old, James, who had difficulty trying new foods—he was happy eating the same foods over and over. He ate healthy food, and he was of a normal weight for his height. However, he couldn't go to birthday parties or stay for dinner at a friend's house because he became very anxious about any food that wasn't familiar, particularly if it was not organic and healthy. James wanted to be able to eat at Chipotle with his friends, and to eat the steak his mother grilled in the summer. His mother wanted him to be able to eat different brands and different toppings on pizza, as well as hot dogs at the baseball games his family loved to attend. Just the thought of hot dogs really upset James, who only wanted to eat healthy, organic food. Here is his hierarchy:

SUDS	Trigger Food
0	Familiar food like noodles, scrambled eggs, quesadillas, etc.
1	
2	A new kind of soup or muffin
3	Beef stew
4	New brand of cheese pizza
5	
6	
7	Steak my mother grilled/pepperoni pizza
8	Chipotle
9	Donut or bacon
10	Hot dog

Elizabeth set homework exposure for the week of eating quinoa, a new kind of muffin, and soup. He thought it would be an easy assignment, about a 2. However, James and his mom first tried tofu soup that they made together, and James could not eat it. They next tried store-bought soup with more success, and made banana chocolate chip muffins, which he also liked. They did not manage to try quinoa.

James was very hard on himself, focusing on his lack of success eating the tofu soup (which his mother said wasn't any good) and not trying quinoa. This was a great opportunity to consider how his thoughts were helping him or not as he worked on exposing himself to the triggers of new foods.

Elizabeth explained to James that his thoughts weren't always accurate or true, which he really enjoyed hearing because he was aware that he was hard on himself in all aspects of his life. She asked him to consider his thoughts when he tried the banana chocolate chip muffins. He found it easy to make up the left-hand side of the list shown below. Then James considered how he could look at these thoughts differently—less emotionally and more rationally. Elizabeth had to help him with this list, but together they came up with a right-hand column that he felt he could believe at least somewhat.

Situation: Eating a banana chocolate chip muffin for the first time	
Cognitive Distortion	**Rational/Neutral Response**
I never ate this before	This is not totally new
It's probably horrible	Don't know; I haven't tried it
It's probably bad for me	Eating some probably won't hurt me
I'm going to starve, there is nothing to eat	If I need to, I can eat more food later
I just want my quesadilla	I can have that another time
Why can't I just have what I want	I am working on eating something new

Particularly notice that we worked on not using reassurance. James's tendency to have all-or-nothing thinking had led him to think that he would starve if he had to eat the muffin and didn't like it, but in his family there wasn't a limit on what he could eat between meals. A different person or an adult might have needed to work on saying "I might starve. That is possible." But as with the example of the therapist in Chapter 5 who said that she failed her client with a bee phobia because she didn't get stung as part of the exposure, it's important to recognize that every client needs individual goals.

Chapter Highlights

- Thoughts are not facts.
- We have choices about how we interpret our thoughts.
- Thoughts can have cognitive distortions we are unaware of.
- Values clarification can help clients find motivation for change.
- Underlying assumptions and core beliefs can get in the way of change.
- Cognitive and behavioral therapy are used together.

TAKE THE NEXT STEP

In your next session with an anxious client, be purposeful about discussing what they value more than anxiety. Develop a strategy for talking back to anxiety, adding this value piece. What did they come up with?

_____

_____

_____

_____

Chapter 8

The Role of Mindfulness in Treating Anxiety and OCD

Mindfulness is "paying attention in a particular way: on purpose, in the present moment, and non-judgmentally."
-Jon Kabat-Zinn

"Don't just do something, sit there."
-Thich Nhat Hanh

When we started practicing as social workers in 1991, the standard approach with anxiety was often to distract a client so that they did not have to experience the intensity of their anxiety symptoms. Distraction is not a current, evidence-based treatment for anxiety and OCD. The problem with distraction is that as long as the person is afraid of their anxious symptoms, they will not teach their brain to handle these uncomfortable feelings. Consequently, they may feel better initially, but in the long run they will continue to be overwhelmed by their anxiety symptoms (Gillihan et al., 2012).

A few years into our careers, therapists started to change the way they taught exposures. Rather than helping their clients avoid anxious feelings, they began to teach them how to accept and tolerate those feelings. During this time, Jon Kabat-Zinn came to the Anxiety Disorders Association of America's (ADAA) annual conference. Those of us who went to his workshop had heard of this approach and were excited to practice with him. I was surprised at how difficult it was to be present with an experience without trying to change it or label it as good or bad! In this chapter, we will be introducing you to some mindfulness concepts that we find to be helpful to people with anxiety or OCD.

Once our clients understand ERP and anxiety tolerance, we begin to practice mindfulness. When they begin to tell us about an anxiety experience, we often ask them, "So what did you do about that?" We hope their response will be, "Nothing." Our Western culture is programmed to do something when we feel discomfort. Doing nothing can feel impossible. So why is teaching mindfulness helpful to our clients?

- It helps clients stay in the present because anxiety is constantly trying to keep us from the present by asking us "what-if" questions about the future or reliving the past.
- It gives the person a different way to look at their anxiety: accept and embrace it rather than resist it.
- It teaches the person self-compassion, acceptance, and the importance of living a valued life.

YOUR TURN

Think of something that was really a challenge for you and created significant distress:

What was your instinctive response?

_____

Imagine yourself doing nothing....What do you think would have happened?

_____

How would you have endured it if you had just allowed it to be?

_____

_____

The following are exercises that you can teach to help your client notice physical sensations and thoughts:

- **Eating a raisin.** When you ask someone to pay attention to their experience with eating a raisin, many people look a bit disgusted because they don't like raisins. This creates a great opportunity to practice handling something that is uncomfortable. Do this with your client and ask them to notice how the raisin tastes, how it feels in their mouth, what it feels like between their teeth, and what thoughts come up as a result of these sensations. Help them to accept their experience, without doing anything to get away from it (either behaviorally or cognitively). They can then go on to practice being present with other tastes while they are eating.

- **Labeling.** We have clients practice saying, "Just (a thought, a worry, an anxious feeling, a sensation)." It is important to say the period out loud at the end of the sentence: "Just a thought, period." Then we ask, "Why do you think saying *just* is helpful?" They usually get it pretty quickly. *Just* minimizes the importance of the experience. We also ask, "Why is saying period at the end important?" Their response is often, "It ends the conversation." Yes! Labeling helps your clients to acknowledge and accept a thought or feeling without getting entangled in the content.

- **Using our senses.** It is helpful for clients with anxiety to stay present in the here and now because anxiety wants to take them to catastrophic places in the future. By paying attention to what they can see, hear, and feel in that moment, they can help to ground themselves in the present. In the office, we often ask clients to describe what they can see for about a minute. Then we ask them to close their eyes and pay attention to what they can hear. After another minute, we ask them to describe what they can feel. This can also be a helpful exercise if they have difficulty falling asleep at night.

- **Noting and describing.** Instead of ruminating with the content of their thoughts, we teach clients to note and describe what is in the physical space around them. Often we will go on a mindful walk, where we don't talk, but we each describe, in our heads, what we are seeing and feeling. We instruct the client to gently, without any judgments, come back to noting and describing their surroundings once they become aware that they are entangled in their thoughts.

- **Breathing.** We always have access to our breath. Sometimes people use breathing in response to anxiety. They may take a big inhale because they feel like they can't get enough oxygen, or they may take several long breaths to try and get the anxiety to go away. With mindful breathing, we teach our clients to use their breath to hold a space for their experience. By connecting to their breath, they can quiet their urge to respond to the anxiety trigger and wait for their wise mind to guide them.

- **Meditation.** Dan Harris, a correspondent for ABC news, had a panic attack while giving the news on national TV. Horrified, he sought treatment and found both CBT and meditation to be the formula that was most helpful for him. Meditation allows us to practice noticing our thoughts and emotions without responding to them. It can be difficult to get an anxious person to begin a meditation practice.

We find it helpful to have them download a meditation app while they are in our office and for us to practice a 10-minute meditation at the end of our sessions. This allows them to process their experience with meditation and helps them to set up a healthy habit for their mind.

The importance of these exercises is that they help your client redefine their relationship with sensations and thoughts. We do this by creating distance between the anxiety trigger and our response. These practices also help us to not get entangled in the anxiety story. As with all other skills, mindfulness is attained through consistent practice.

YOUR TURN

Choose one of the mindfulness exercises to practice daily for one week and note your experience:

Which practice did you choose?

_____

_____

_____

Did have any difficulty getting started or being consistent?

_____

_____

_____

What obstacles did you experience (both internal and external)?

_____

_____

_____

What was your experience the first time you did the practice versus the last time you did the practice?

_____

_____

_____

How likely are you to continue this practice?

_____

_____

_____

Choose another mindfulness practice and pay attention to your experience using the above questions.

MINDFULNESS AND ANXIETY

Anxiety wants people to catastrophize about the future or fret about the past. But the only thing that exists is the present. Difficult thoughts and feelings, while being uncomfortable, are not dangerous. Allowing these feelings and thoughts to come and go is a helpful approach with anxiety. Some scientists say we have over 50,000 thoughts a day. Anxious people tend to become attached to their thoughts and play them over and over. Just because we have a thought doesn't make it true. Learning how to notice a thought without believing it will be very beneficial.

Resisting anxiety will only make it stronger. You've heard the saying, "The more you resist, the more it persists." This couldn't be more true with anxiety. It is instinctual for us to try to get away from something that is painful or difficult. Mindfulness can help anxious people learn to accept and allow. We keep Chinese handcuffs in our office and ask people to put their fingers in them and try to get them out. This is a great way to demonstrate this concept to your clients.

Loving kindness is a powerful tool when treating anxiety. Anxious people are very good at feeling shame and criticizing themselves when things don't go well. Pay attention to this when you work with your clients. It is so automatic for them to turn on themselves right in front of you! Think of how often they are punishing themselves for having difficult thoughts or giving in to their compulsions when you are not around. Remember, mindfulness means being nonjudgmental. We like to have clients put their hand over their heart, rub in a circular motion, and say, "Even though I (e.g., gave into my anxiety), I love and accept myself." Self-compassion not only feels good, but it helps quiet the part of the brain that is being overactive. Loving-kindness meditations are also helpful. Loving-kindness meditations are a great way to develop kindness towards ourselves and others. It involves mentally sending kind thoughts and compassion towards others by silently repeating a series of mantras.

Chapter Highlights

- Mindfulness is being present, in the moment, without judgment.
- Mindfulness teaches us how to be observers of our anxiety.
- Mindfulness helps us to accept and allow anxiety rather than resist it.
- Practicing mindfulness daily using the techniques in this chapter will support cognitive behavioral therapy for anxiety and OCD.
- Loving kindness toward oneself quiets the stress response.

TAKE THE NEXT STEP

1. Keep raisins in your office to practice noticing sensations and thoughts with your clients.
2. Purchase some Chinese handcuffs on the Internet. Play with them yourself and then use them with your clients to teach the effects of resistance.
3. Think of something that you did today, that you feel frustrated or disappointed about. Put your hand over your heart chakra and circle it, saying, "Even though (this happened), I love and accept myself." How did that feel to you?

   _____

   _____

4. Go to YouTube and listen to a loving-kindness or compassion meditation. Practice it by yourself and then with a client. What did you notice?

   _____

5. Give the following exercise to your client as homework and discuss at their next session.

···
The Mindfulness of Breath

In this exercise, you will have a chance to practice a basic mindfulness skill—noticing your breath. Record this script and then play it back for yourself. Notice how the calm or pressure in your voice changes the experience. Try having a loved one record it for you to feel their support and encouragement as you work on this new skill.

1. Close your eyes or allow your gaze to rest softly on a spot on the floor in front of you.

2. Notice where you feel the breath in your body and allow your attention to rest in this spot. It may be in your belly, the back of your throat, or your nostrils.

3. Keep your focus on your breath, noticing the sensation of your breath as you breathe in and as you breathe out. Imagine you are riding the waves of your own breathing.

4. Each time you notice that your mind has wandered off the breath, gently bring your attention back to the place you feel your breath.

5. Each time your mind wanders, all you need to do is gently bring it back to your breath, again and again.

6. If you notice thoughts that you aren't doing this right or you aren't good at it, just notice them and again gently bring your attention back to your breath. These are just thoughts; they don't mean you aren't doing it right.

7. If you notice uncomfortable feelings, just notice them without labeling them as good or bad. Return to your breath and ride the wave.

Chapter 9

Cognitive Behavioral Therapy with Kids

Anxiety disorders are the most common mental health problem in children and youth, diagnosed in 5–18% of people before the age of 18. Most anxiety disorders start in childhood; the average age of onset is 11. We love working with children because we know we may be helping prevent a life-long problem from being established. We know that prevention works.

Treatment with CBT for children is important to prevent anxiety or OCD from becoming a part of the way the child sees him or herself. Untreated children often fall behind their peers socially and academically as they have increased school absences and often avoid extracurricular activities.

The same CBT philosophy you have been reading about throughout this workbook—tolerating distress and uncertainty and developing resilience—works well with children once translated into age-appropriate metaphors and games. CBT, medication, or a combination of the two are all effective treatment (James, Soler, & Weatherall, 2005). However, children have the potential to learn quickly once they are taught CBT with ERP, so we often wait to add medication unless they are not functioning in their life or not making progress in therapy.

AGES AND DIAGNOSES

When evaluating a child for anxiety or OCD, keep in mind that the experience is different at different life stages. Anxiety is cruel and comes after what any of us fears most. Younger children's fears are quite different from the fears of adolescents. We often hear from clinicians about how to distinguish normal, age-appropriate fears from anxiety or OCD, and it really comes down to *intensity*, *avoidance*, and *suffering*. Normal, age-appropriate fears can be intense—don't get us wrong—but usually a child is comforted by a parent or adult and moves on to other thoughts or activities.

Children with anxiety and OCD will be unable to move on, and will try to avoid the trigger as best as they can. The suffering in these children can be difficult to watch. They are so afraid of the trigger that it often feels like a very real threat to them.

We think about a 10-year-old boy who was terrified of going up to his bedroom when no one else was upstairs. He was intensely ashamed of this fear, and had been punished by his parents several times for not going to bed on time before they learned that he was phobic of being upstairs alone and that was the reason for his refusal to go upstairs. The fear felt wrong to him—it was "ego-dystonic," meaning it didn't fit with his overall view of himself.

Another client, a girl, was 12 and terrified of vomiting, which has a special name, *emetophobia*. This girl felt completely justified by her fear of vomiting, but she did notice that her friends weren't as fearful as she was, so she hid her fears from them. This led to her avoiding social situations like sleepovers where she might get triggered and be unable to be with her mother.

We think of a 17-year-old with pervasive fears of talking to peers, though he related well to adults. He had a few friends in ninth and tenth grades, but by junior year was isolated and eventually refused to go to school.

He felt defective, like he just didn't get what everyone else knew automatically about being able to talk to people his age.

The onset of OCD falls into two distinct age groups—5–8 years old and adolesence. Since it still takes on average 14–17 years for people with OCD to get the correct diagnosis and treatment, it's important to take a look at how different OCD looks in these different age groups.

Young children in the first age group may have habits or fears that seem odd. A 6-year-old was terrified of being poisoned by cleaning products, and so would bring a small, dirty rag to school and wipe his chair down before he would sit on it. He only ate from a specific plate at home and had to have his lunch packed just so. If his mom forgot to pack the lunch the way he felt safe with, he would not eat.

You may remember our earlier story about an 8-year-old girl who had a sudden fear that she had eaten something not food, like gasoline when she was in her booster seat when her mom pumped gas. Or her jacket zipper when she zipped her coat at recess.

These types of fears go far beyond simply lining up similar items like cars or shoes or saying a prayer in a specific way for a few nights. These children were inconsolable if forced to do something they felt was dangerous, and no amount of reassurance from their parents about the impossibility of their fears was able to calm them.

OCD in an adolescent can take an existential form as it did for a 17-year-old who spent hours talking to his best friend about if he was really here and really experiencing the emotion that he thought he felt. His grades, understandably, had dropped with the onset of OCD because he was consumed by figuring out what felt to him like vitally important questions. A modified version of the Yale-Brown Obsessive Compulsive Scale (YBOCS), the CYBOCS, is helpful when evaluating children who have OCD. You can find it online, and use it to track improvement over time.

Notice in all these examples—from social anxiety to simple phobia to OCD—how the symptoms and focus of the problem are specific to the developmental stage of the child. Children can get stuck developmentally by anxiety and OCD and so can seem younger than they are.

CBT WORKS IN CHILDREN AND ADOLESCENTS

Fortunately, CBT has been found to work well for children and adolescents, and is the recommended first-line treatment. A research paper with the wonderful title, "Evidence Base Update: 50 Years of Research on Treatment for Child and Adolescent Anxiety," notes that CBT improves functioning and reduces symptoms, and furthermore that treatment is flexible, so it can be tailored to specific difficulties the child is experiencing (Higa-McMillan, Francis, Rith-Najarian, & Chorpita, 2016). Treatment works best when CBT is a collaboration with the child, not when exposure is forced. Getting to that collaboration, when the child willingly participates in exposures that are triggering, is the magic of working with children.

ENGAGE CHILDREN AND PARENTS IN TREATMENT

Children and adolescents who come for help with anxiety and OCD are typically suffering and missing out on important activities and experiences. As with all CBT, good therapy involves a primary focus on empathizing with this suffering to build an alliance between the child and the therapist. Interestingly, the more the child or adolescent feels they have a good alliance with their therapist, the better they do with being involved with their treatment (McLeod et al., 2014).

Engaging children and parents, like engaging adults, takes getting them on board with the diagnosis, the scope of the problem, and understanding the anxious brain. Of course, it's important to use child-friendly language. It can be helpful to have the child give their anxiety a name. One client called it "mond"—half monster and half friend. Once named, parents, siblings, and teachers can all call it mond instead of anxiety or OCD.

Very young children—or people of any age who have disabilities that make writing hard—will do better to have an adult notetaker, or to draw pictures or make collages to understand the problem. The child who had a fear of being upstairs without his parents, for example, had a learning disability that made reading and writing hard, so even though he was 10 years old, they drew pictures and Elizabeth made charts for him to fill in rather than having him write himself. He drew an especially funny picture of a brain chasing him up the stairs, which helped him with that all-important recognition that it wasn't *him* who was frightened, it was his mean, anxious brain that was scaring him.

We also constructed Lego stairs and used Lego people to climb up and down the stairs. His parents, in the room with us for the appointment, were fascinated by our work. This approach taught them that asking him, "Why are you scared to be upstairs?" was not helping him progress. This is never a good question! The child is frightened because he is triggered. It's not logical—it is because the brain says it is scary.

Young children aren't going to understand much about the brain, but running through the explanation for the parents is vital, because parents play such an important role in helping the child see that they can tolerate situations and feelings. If parents understand that this is a brain glitch, they can convey that to their child in tough moments. Make sure to set aside a section of the notebook for parents to write in—we use a Post-it Note as a flag for that section and invite them to write their concerns or questions, and later compliments on exposures done well! Parents and kids of all ages enjoy the analogy of the burned toast setting off the fire alarm —it's a false alarm, not a signal of actual danger.

TAILOR TREATMENT BY AGE AND DEVELOPMENTAL ABILITY

Children with anxiety come in all ages and abilities. Consider not only the chronological age, but the learning differences or developmental challenges of children when deciding how to connect best (Kendall & Peterman, 2015).

Parents are generally a big asset to treatment, and one of the most important parts of psychoeducation is to ally the parent and child in working together on the problem of anxiety. The team—therapist, client, and parent—is crucial. Keep in mind, though, that parents may have anxiety, too.

We think of a girl that Elizabeth worked with on social anxiety. Using a different phobia or anxiety problem to illustrate a point is often very helpful for children who generally like the idea of being able to help others. In explaining how exposure would work, Elizabeth used an example of a child with a spider phobia and put her laminated pictures of spiders on the floor between them. The girl, who had been very quiet, burst into laughter and pointed to her mother, who had pulled her feet onto her chair to get away from the pictures. Elizabeth pulled out another blank notebook and had this girl help her mother get it started using her own as a blueprint. This happens all the time in treatment. We like to normalize this experience, and remind our clients that we can all learn from each other in a family—learning doesn't always go from parent to child!

Client Age	Parents in the Room?	Special Focus of CBT Therapy/ERP
Infant–4 years	Yes	Play; teach parents techniques for home
5–8	Yes	Drawing, playing, and acting
9–12	Sometimes	"Scientific" approach, usually all writing
13–17	Usually at end	Self-identity; values clarification

YOUR TURN

What examples of children with anxiety or OCD from your practice come to mind?

_____

_____

_____

GOAL SETTING AND REWARDS

It is crucial to successful work with children and adolescents to find goals that are important to them. Everyone does better working toward goals that matter to them directly.

The 17-year-old with social anxiety who was out of school was a hockey fan, and had a goal of going to watch the team practice. Sure, it was important to get him back to school. However, he felt so far from that goal, and had been out of school and on home and hospital instruction for so long, that just getting him out of the house was a reasonable first goal. The photo of himself at a hockey practice that he brought in to our next session was priceless—we didn't know he could smile like that. That gave him the confidence to take the hard steps it took to get back to school. This exposure, going to a hockey practice, had a great built-in reward. For younger kids, small toys or chips or stickers toward larger treats work well.

We like to ask parents and kids to brainstorm together what rewards fit with their family, since for some families, going out for ice cream or ordering pizza is reasonable. In one family we worked with, the child was working toward the very large reward of getting a puppy, which the parents had wanted to get once they saw that the child was well enough to help with the training. It is important to instruct the parents to give rewards when a child practices their exposures. If they promise, but don't deliver (which happens frequently), it is not very rewarding.

POSSIBLE REWARDS

Family pizza night

Small toys

Extra time with a parent (reading, etc.)

Going bowling with a friend

Going to a movie with a friend

A new book

A family game night

New game for the computer or phone

Something toward a hobby or activity—like seeds to plant a garden or a new baseball bat

Extra screen time

A trip to an amusement park

YOUR TURN

What rewards do you use successfully with children and adolescents?

• Toys in your office you can give out

_____

- Treats parents agree to give

  _____

- IOUs from parents for special events like bowling

  _____

- Games you play with the child as a reward for exposures

  _____

- Other

  _____

ESTABLISH HIERARCHY AND START ERP

A hierarchy for a young child may be simple, however, the usual barrier to starting exposure successfully is finding an easier step. Both of us having done this work for 25 years, we can say confidently that there is always an easier step to start with. Clients and parents don't get how to do this, so this is one of the most important parts of your early work with your clients.

Think about the 10-year-old with the fear of going upstairs alone. To him, there was only one possible item on his hierarchy: going upstairs alone. That was a fine place to start, so it was added to his hierarchy as a 10. But what about drawing a picture of a child going upstairs? This wasn't scary to him, so we recorded drawing a picture as a 2. What about having his mother stand at the bottom of the stairs while he sat on the top step and sang her a song? Or recording himself telling a story of going upstairs and being scared but staying? By the time we finished, we had a nice long list to work from.

If parents are going to be part of exposures at home, it is crucial to start ERP in session with your client and parents. This can be in vivo, play, or imagination exposure. The key is to have the child voluntarily do something that triggers their anxiety or OCD.

You want to be there the first time to help:

- Be a cheerleader.
- Acknowledge that it is hard.
- Give the child credit for attempting the work even if it is a small step.

This last point is crucial, because often parents and anxious children do not give credit for small steps, which then makes it almost impossible to tackle harder exposure.

YOUR TURN

What goal does a child you are working with have that seems all-or-nothing?

_____

_____

Now that you have read this example of creating new, easier tasks, can you come up with some new possibilities for this exposure?

_____

_____

_____

AGE-APPROPRIATE EXPLANATIONS OF COGNITIVE RESTRUCTURING

Young children may not developmentally be able to understand much about the brain or cognitive restructuring, but almost everyone gets the idea that you are helping the child to learn brain training. Practicing the piano, practicing spelling words, or practicing drills in soccer are all possible examples that might help a child recognize that just like every other activity, to get better at being able to do the things they fear, they need to practice them.

Conceptualizing anxiety as a brain trick or a bully—and helping the child learn to boss back the brain bully—is another explanation that is appropriate to all ages of kids. This is especially important as so many anxious children are rule followers, and are being obedient and following the rules of their anxiety. The parent will need to help reinforce that they do not need to be nice to a bully. It's quite fun to have the child draw a picture of the anxiety as they personify it (monster, dragon, etc.), put it on the floor in front of all of you, and take turns bossing back the anxiety:

"You can make me feel bad, but you can't make me stay home."

"You are just a big bully."

"This stinks, but I can handle it."

"You got me that time, but I'm going to try again."

"You can't stop me from doing what I want."

The metaphor of dipping a toe in a cold swimming pool at the beginning of the summer helps kids recognize that they can tackle one part of the anxiety at a time, not have to face the whole thing, and also that if they do need to face the whole thing, do it in a way that is fast and effective—jump into the cold swimming pool! We want kids and parents to recognize that those moments of high anxiety are not bad—they are simply more opportunities to practice new attitudes.

SPECIAL CONSIDERATIONS FOR TEENS

Sometimes it is important to work with teens without parents in the session for at least some of the time. This is especially true for socially anxious or separation-anxiety teens who need the opportunity you will provide in sessions to set goals and session agendas without feedback from parents. Many anxious teens typically do not have enough practice with agenda setting and being away from their parents in the rest of their lives. Try having the parent come in for the last 15 minutes of the session and have the teen lead the conversation by summarizing what you did and demonstrating any new exposures or cognitive reframing they learned.

WORKING WITH SCHOOLS

When working with children, you may have to partner with the staff at the their school to make sure everyone is on the same page. It is helpful to ask for a meeting where the teachers, guidance counselor, school nurse, school psychologist, and principal are in attendance. We also invite the parents and child (depending on their age and capabilities) to attend. In this meeting and future communications, it will be important to educate everyone about anxiety, discuss specifically how this student is struggling in school, and develop a treatment plan that helps them to conquer their fears in school. You can use the following handout to educate school staff on helpful ways to talk with an anxious student.

Accommodations, while sometimes helpful in the beginning, need to be closely monitored so that the student is eventually facing their fears and learning how to tolerate the thoughts and feelings, while slowly removing accommodations. In this meeting, we ask the student to share their struggles and what they have learned about getting better. We also explain to the teachers how to coach a student through an anxiety episode.

SCHOOL REFUSAL

Kids need to be in school—it is the place where they learn academically and socially. This is not a debate about homeschooling, but rather a recognition that, for most kids with anxiety, school is especially important because it gives them a structured place to normalize anxious thoughts and feelings surrounded by peers and supportive adults. Kids who are home from school due to anxiety will need help to get back to a regular day. Look at http://www.WorryWiseKids.org for a great sample list of accommodations that may be helpful as a child begins CBT.

As always with accommodations, it is not intended to be a long-term solution, but rather a step in the process of returning to school. Usually, it is best to start with the child returning to school for a partial day, often the first few classes of the day—waiting until later in the day gives anxiety more time to talk the child out of attending. Help the child come up with what to say to other kids who may ask why they have been out of school, and help the teachers come up with a reasonable expectation for the child to catch up with missed work. Often, being back in school is much more important than completing every assignment.

Anxiety in the School: *Tips for Teachers*

1. Validate the child's feelings and help them to identify it as anxiety.

   "You are feeling yucky right now, are you worried about something?"

   "It's normal to feel anxious before a test or speaking in front of the class."

2. Do **not** reassure an anxious child.

   "You'll be fine."

   "You always do well on a test."

   "You don't have anything to worry about."

   "The day will be over before you know it."

3. Help the child to tolerate his/her uncomfortable feelings.

   "I know you're feeling pretty bad right now, but I wonder if you can sit at your seat while you're feeling bad and I'll check in with you in a few minutes."

   "You really miss your mom this morning. It will be hard, but I bet you can get started with your work even though you miss her and you might find that working helps those feelings to quiet down a little."

   "The storm outside is making you feel very scared. I'm wondering how many of you can work even though you're feeling scared."

4. Be a cheerleader for them as they tolerate their anxious feelings.

   "I am so proud of you for finishing your work even though you were feeling anxious!"

   "You did a great job of staying in school today even though you missed your mom!"

   "I really appreciate how hard you must have worked to not ask me questions all day even though you might have been worried about doing your work correctly."

5. Challenge him/her to go for longer periods of time or to do something that will make them feel worse (after they begin to feel empowered).

   "You worked really hard at staying in the class for the last 15 minutes even though you wanted to go to the nurse's office. Can you work hard for another 15 minutes?"

   "You completed that portion of the test even though you felt anxious. I'm wondering if you can feel anxious and do the next part of the test."

6. Help them to see that when they do something even though they feel anxious, their anxiety eventually quiets down.

7. Reward very anxious children with small tokens, candy, or prizes for completing tasks that make them feel anxious. (Use lots of praise for older children.)

8. Remember, children will not learn to tolerate anxiety if they do not practice the skill. They need your encouragement to sit with the bad feelings and work anyway. If you reassure them or send them to the nurses office, they will only learn that they can't tolerate these feelings and the anxiety will worsen.

Chapter Highlights

- Anxiety disorders are the most common mental health disorder in children and teens.
- Anxiety is differentiated from normal, age-appropriate fears in intensity, avoidance and suffering.
- CBT is effective in children and teens, and is the first-line treatment.
- Therapy works best when children are engaged in treatment, not when they are forced.
- Treatment can be tailored to age and developmental level.
- Review rewards with the family before beginning ERP to increase compliance.
- Establish a hierarchy using small, manageable steps to get started.

TAKE THE NEXT STEP

What are your obstacles to working with children who experience anxiety or OCD?

_____

_____

_____

Based on what you learned in this chapter, what can you do differently to begin to develop more confidence in your work with children with anxiety or OCD?

_____

_____

_____

Game Ideas

Use the following games as ideas when you work with kids. Be sure to check SUDS levels (0–10).

1. **Monster Stomp**: The child writes their fears on 8″ × 11″ paper (one per paper). The child pretends they are a monster by jumping on one of the papers and stating out loud a healthy response to the fear. They continue to jump on each fear (piece of paper) until they have developed healthy responses to the fears. This game helps them to stop feeling like a victim of their fears and to develop healthy ways to talk to their fears.

2. **Basketball**: Have the child write their fears or bad thoughts on different pieces of paper. Get a hoop or garbage can. Have the child read their fear aloud, crumble the paper, and shoot a basket. This game helps them to say their fears out loud and change the emotion.

3. **Matching**: Write down the child's fears two times on different pieces of paper. Mix up the fears and play a matching game with the child. This helps the child be playful with their fears.

4. **Ball Toss**: Get a ball or bean bag and toss it to the child while saying something bad that will happen to them based on what they fear will happen. The child then passes the ball or bag to you and says something bad that will happen to you. You can change this depending on the content of the child's superstitious or fear thoughts. For example, Jon worries that bad things will happen to his Mom while he is in school. His therapist is helping Jon to see that just because he has these thoughts doesn't make them true. She plays pass the ball with him by first starting out tossing it to him and saying, "It is going to storm today." He catches the ball and says, "I think there will be an earthquake." She catches the ball and says, "Maybe I'll get sick." He catches the ball and says, "Maybe my Mom will get sick." They continue to toss the ball back and forth saying increasingly anxiety-provoking thoughts. Playing a game with worries helps children see that we can't predict what will happen. It also helps them practice tolerating thoughts and feelings associated with their thoughts.

5. **Magical Thinking Game**: Start by saying, "The picture will fall off the wall." Then the child chooses something in your office and says, "The _____ will fall over." Continue to do this, adding more frightening fears/thoughts that the child is concerned about (e.g., "My mom will die today," "I will vomit," "There will be a tornado tomorrow."). This helps the child realize that thoughts are not linked to actions.

6. **Rate Your Vomit**: Go to http://RateMyVomit.com and rate vomit pictures with a child who has a fear of vomiting.

7. **Talk Back to Anxiety:** Use the blank cartoon on the following page to have your client illustrate their fears and talk back to me. For example, Box 1, Anxiety Says: "What if you throw up?" Box 2, I Say Back: "No I won't throw up." Box 3, Anxiety Talks Louder: "How do you know? Sammy threw up yesterday!" Box 4, I Get Stronger: "I might throw up, I don't care." Box 5, I Get Even Stronger: "Throwing up isn't worse than the way you make me feel every day even when I don't throw up." and Box 6, I Get Strongest Yet: "I hope I do throw up so you stop bothering me." Make a copy of page 93 and have your client write those answers in the correct boxes. If they can, draw a stick figure (or a real character if you can draw!) and see how powerful the message is.

Talk Back To Anxiety

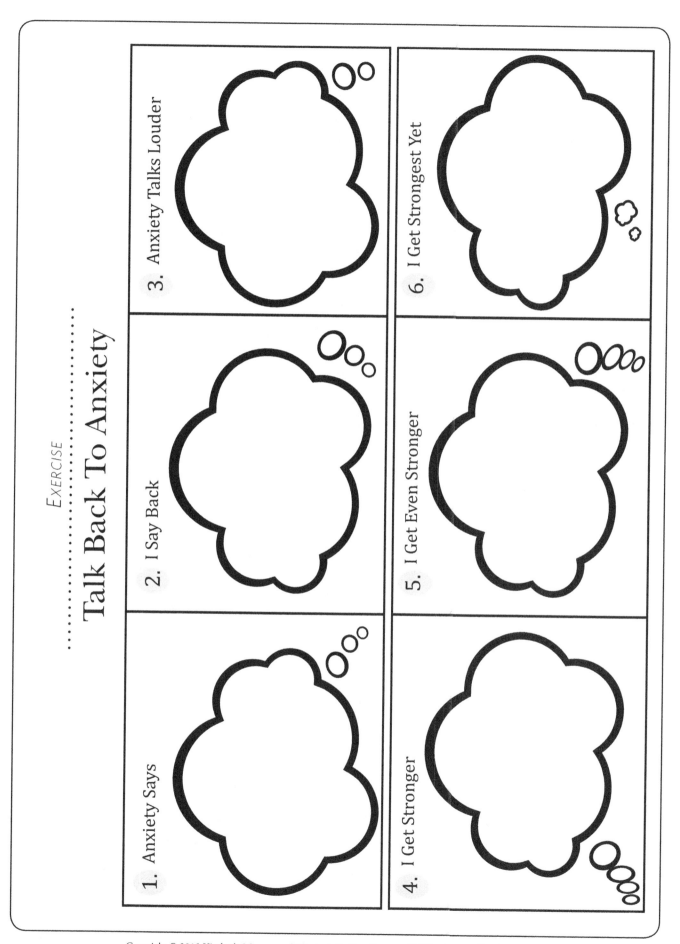

1. Anxiety Says

2. I Say Back

3. Anxiety Talks Louder

4. I Get Stronger

5. I Get Even Stronger

6. I Get Strongest Yet

Chapter 10

Cognitive Behavioral Therapy for OCD

Obsessive compulsive disorder can often be both challenging and scary for a clinician to treat. The concepts of CBT with exposure and response prevention make sense until you have to figure out how to use it with themes and triggers that may create disgust in you and shame in your client.

Kimberly was recently working with a man who was married and had a 5-year-old son. He had some anxiety that waxed and waned throughout his life, yet was always manageable. Recently, he had seen a story on television that involved a father shooting his son with his rifle. The son died. This affected her client deeply. He found himself filled with anxiety and worry about possibly doing the same thing to his son.

He had great difficulty sharing his fears with Kimberly, but she was able to help him feel safe enough after explaining the anxious brain to him and sharing some examples of fear stories that we hear every day. He told her he had images of blowing his son's head off. He told her frequently, he would never want to do that, but was uncertain if he actually would. He was in the process of selling all of his hunting rifles. He begged his wife every night to reassure him that he would never harm his son. However, the thoughts and images only grew stronger with time.

OCD consists of obsessions and compulsions. Obsessions are images, thoughts, or fears that create a tremendous amount of anxiety. These obsessions are often the opposite of who the person is and play on a vulnerability they have. Compulsions are the behaviors or rituals they engage in to get away from the thought or neutralize the intensity of the feeling. These compulsions can be mental or physical.

Mental rituals might consist of praying that they would never do the thing they fear, or saying the opposite of what they thought, or visualizing checking something instead of actually checking. Another important aspect of OCD is the client's ability to distinguish that the thoughts are not "real." Often, the client will say something like, "I know I would never do this, but I can't stop thinking that I might." This means the thoughts are ego-dystonic and this is helpful to the therapist in identifying OCD. Sometimes children are unable to identify their thoughts as being separate from themselves.

YOUR TURN

Identify which thoughts might be OCD and which are something else. Label as O (OCD), U (Uncertain), N (Not OCD). Answers appear at the end of the chapter.

1. ___I hate being dirty!
2. ___I can handle dirt as long as I can wash it off at the end of the day; otherwise I won't be able to sleep.
3. ___I know I'm straight, but every time I look at my best friend I think I'm gay, but I know I'm not.
4. ___I think I'm bisexual; I'm not sure whether I like being with men or women.
5. ___Sometimes I get so angry at my kids I feel like I could hit them!

6. ___I keep having thoughts of smothering my child, so I'm afraid to even hug them.

7. ___I often fantasize about kidnapping someone and torturing them.

8. ___What if I blurt something out that offends God? I'm afraid I'll go to hell.

9. ___I don't think I believe in God.

10. ___I have a problem with remembering to lock the doors or to unplug things when I leave the house.

11. ___I worry so much about leaving things unplugged that I have had to leave work and come home to check.

EVALUATING AND DIAGNOSING OCD

Obsessive compulsive disorder can be sometimes challenging to evaluate and diagnose for a couple of reasons. First, the content of the obsessions can make any clinician wonder if the client might really act on their fears. Kimberly teaches psychiatric residents about diagnosing OCD. After she explains the difference between ego-syntonic (thoughts and feelings that are consistent with their sense of self) and ego-dystonic (thoughts and feelings that are in conflict or dissonant with their sense of self), we discuss clients who come to the emergency room with the fear of killing themselves or someone else. For the safety of everyone, psychiatrists often hospitalize these people without thoroughly assessing for OCD. Someone who has the fear of harm will be using the hospitalization to protect themselves and others, saying something like, "I don't want to kill myself or anyone, but I can't stop thinking I might. I just want to be in the hospital, where I know I'll be safe."

Another reason it can be difficult to evaluate OCD is that there are often many forms and manifestations of the obsessions and compulsions, so that it can often feel overwhelming to get a good grasp of all of the symptoms. We ask clients to bring a list of their triggers and what they do to feel better. People with OCD can bring in a two-page, single-spaced list, which can feel overwhelming to us and the client!

We utilize the Yale-Brown Obsessive Compulsive Scale (YBOCS). With this scale, you can identify their obsessions and compulsions, both current and past. You can also assess the severity of symptoms and re-evaluate the severity of their symptoms periodically. You and your clients will love to see their progress.

YOUR TURN

Download the YBOCS and make copies to have ready to use with your clients. (See website in reference section)

FACE IT, FEEL IT, AND DO THE OPPOSITE

One of the mantras we use when treating anxiety is "face it and feel it." The defining characteristics of treating anxiety are the client's ability to face the uncertainty of the situation that is triggering their fear and to ride out the accompanying anxiety until it passes.

With OCD, we add one more part to this saying: "Do the opposite." This can be bewildering to your client, as they have spent all of their time doing exactly what OCD tells them. Psychoeducation can be helpful here.

Explain to your client that OCD often messes with them in a way that is the opposite of who they are. Because they care so much about what OCD is telling them, they do whatever is necessary to make sure that thing isn't true or doesn't happen. We often use the metaphor of a bully. The bully tries to hurt us around things we are most vulnerable about. We often give in to the bully by trying to do what it says, hoping that it won't keep messing with us. However, doing exactly the opposite is the best way to teach a bully to stop messing with you. Showing the bully that you can handle its taunts is the most powerful tool you have.

Kimberly often uses the example of a bully telling her that she looks stupid in glasses, because she has worn glasses for a long time and wishes she didn't need to. If she listened to the bully, she might not wear her glasses the next time she saw him, which would encourage the bully to mess with her even more. However, if she wore a flashier pair of glasses, looked the bully in the eye and said, "Go ahead, say whatever you want, I can handle it!," the bully would lose his or her power. Kimberly has a client who took a leave from college because she developed OCD about illness her first semester. She avoided being around people because they might be sick. She also developed detailed cleaning rituals to make sure she was not in contact with any viruses. Once Kimberly educated her about her disorder and explained Face It, Feel It, and Do the Opposite, she started purposely seeking people out and asking them a question. She also began to not check her laundry to see if she put detergent in the machine. Instead she said, "I may or may not have put detergent in. I hope I didn't put detergent in so I can practice feeling anxious and teaching my brain to handle it!"

Remember that anticipatory anxiety is the most powerful way your brain has to prevent you from doing the opposite. Educate your clients about this and have them notice their SUDS score before, during, and after the exposure. If they are struggling to do the opposite, have them come up with a way to talk to their amygdala so that they can be more successful.

YOUR TURN

List an opposite behavior that might go along with some of the following obsessions and compulsions:

Obsession/Compulsion	Opposite
Praying to have OCD taken away.	
Changing to clean clothes after school or work.	
Fearing that you said something to offend someone.	
Having spouse make dinner to avoid contamination.	
Worrying about illnesses and calling the doctor.	
Spending a long time with a project so that you don't miss anything.	
Reviewing how you interacted with a child to make sure you didn't do anything inappropriate.	

IN VIVO EXPOSURE THERAPY

In vivo exposure therapy is the form of CBT that allows people to reduce the fear associated with their triggers. There are two forms of exposure therapy: real and imagined. Real in vivo exposure consists of creating artificial experiences where your client can practice being triggered and facing their fears in real time. It is important to develop a trigger list and rank-order their triggers from least anxiety-provoking to most anxiety-provoking. You will start with the least anxiety-provoking trigger and develop ERP with your client's guidance. It is normal for a client to think they can do something and not be able to, or to believe they can't do something when they really can. This is why it is important to set up an exposure in a way that will help your client experience success, no matter how seemingly small the exposure is.

Kimberly had a client, a teenage boy who was afraid he got HIV after kissing a girl. He was too ashamed to talk about this and was only able to say, "I know what I'm thinking isn't even true, but I can't stop freaking out about it!" She tried her best to have him tell her the content of his fear so they could develop ERP, but he was unable to. So this became the exposure before the exposure. We try very hard never to give in to a client's fear.

After many attempts to share the content, he was only able to agree to text Kimberly the first letter of the first word after he got out to his car. However, once he took this first tiny step, she was able to celebrate his success in a text back to him and ask him to be even more courageous by sending the rest of the content. At their next session, they began ERP on this fear. (See Chapter 5 for more information about exposure therapy.)

Sometimes with OCD treatment, we have to use imagined exposure, because we are unable to expose our clients to the thing that they fear. Examples of this are the following: a client who believes she had an abortion 20 years ago and believes she will go to hell for it; a mother who fears she will harm her children by chopping them up with a knife; a teenager who fears bringing an assault rifle to school; a woman who is convinced she will die from cancer.

When fears and compulsions exist in people's minds (often called "pure O"), imaginal exposures are helpful. Clients who tell you that they don't engage in any compulsions, or tell you they have pure O, often don't realize that they actually engage in mental compulsions.

One form of imaginal exposure is to write a script. Scripts consist of writing or recording the client's OCD nightmare, including an ending that is their worst fear. This often gives you an idea of how your client is vulnerable in this area. Initially, the therapist will help a client write a script. The goal is for the client to be able to write scripts on their own to use when they are no longer in therapy. Often, starting with the client experiencing their fear is too much, so model your own bravery and put yourself into the script as a first step So, for a client who is terrified to drive on the highway because she imagines being in a crash and dying in a fiery wreck, we start with "My therapist is driving home after this session and is in a crash. She dies in a fiery wreck." This does several important things—it allows your client to experience the image with *you* not *themselves* or the people they care about, and also shows your willingness to allow terrible thoughts into your own mind.

Scripts can be powerful. For example, we had a client who didn't hug her children for fear of harming them. When she recorded her worst nightmare, the ending was, "and I left the house without a care in the world." That was important information for us. This was a woman who cared deeply, and OCD was trying to convince her that she didn't care about harming her children. The more she tried to convince herself that she did care and she would never harm them, the worse her symptoms got. Later in vivo exposures included her saying, "I may or may not care if I harm my children, but I am going to hug my child because that is what mothers do."

Once your client writes an exposure script, their homework is to read it over and over or record it and listen over and over until their SUDS level decreases to 50% of its original number. Imaginal exposures can be powerful experiences for your client. It helps them see their thoughts for what they are: just thoughts.

The woman who was afraid she didn't care if she harmed her children read her script three times into her phone to record it and listen to it later. The first time, she wept while she read the script and paused to catch her breath several times. The second time, she was able to read it without pausing, but still cried. The third time, she did not pause or cry. In fact, she embellished the story with even more descriptions of her killings. She said that the script was the most powerful part of her therapy.

YOUR TURN

1. Write a script of your worst nightmare, being as descriptive as possible and ending with your worst fear. Read this over and over until you feel a shift in your emotional attachment to the story.

2. Write down "I hope (someone you adore) dies a painful death this week." Carry this paper with you today and sleep with it under your pillow until you can handle carrying those thoughts with you and are not connecting to the content. Your emotional distress should also quiet but it may not.

Imaginal Script for OCD

Our thoughts are just that—thoughts. Yet we can spend so much energy trying to push a thought away that we instead pay way more attention to then we intended. In this exercise, welcome an unpleasant thought. Purposely think this unpleasant thought and then instead of retreating from it, stick with it. What happens to your SUDS level? Does it go down as you allow the thought to be there without resistance?

Fear: I will be responsible for something bad happening.

I love taking care of animals. I am currently fostering a dog named Snickers, and just received a phone call that someone wants to adopt him. I am feeling anxious about this. How will I know it's a good family for him? What if they hurt him? I agree to meet the family, but have to hurry because I have to be at work in an hour. They seem okay. I don't want to give up this dog, but I know I have to. I am only a foster family.

The family comes to pick up Snickers the next day and I get this strange feeling in my gut. I am not sure this is the right family, but I have nothing to go on. They take Snickers with them and I feel horrible. I don't sleep that night worrying that I gave this dog to a family who may harm him. I call off work the next day because I can't stop crying. How could I be so reckless? I spent such little time with the adoptive family. I'll never know if they were the right one or if they are being mean to Snickers.

Assignment: Read this script over and over until your SUDS level decreases by 50%. Continue to read this script several times a day until your initial SUDS level is below a 5.

Do's and Don'ts of OCD Treatment

OCD can be a challenging and intimidating disorder to treat, but so very rewarding! Here is a list of do's and don'ts that will help you and your client experience success.

Do:

- Start with a trigger list.
- Develop a hierarchy.
- Start with the least anxiety-provoking theme and trigger within the theme.
- Involve and educate family and friends to be coaches. (See Chapter 6.)
- Be a team with your client to develop exposures.
- Ask what obstacles they might experience when practicing ERP.
- Practice ERP in session so you can identify behaviors and thoughts that may prevent success during an exposure at home.
- Start small and go smaller, if necessary. It doesn't matter how small the exposure is as long as they are successful and learn to ride out the wave of fear or anxiety.
- Increase the intensity of the exposure once they have successfully handled the previous exposure.
- Come up with ways to talk back to OCD and not give in to the fears.
- Have your client practice exposures consistently, frequently, and intensely to have the best chance of recovery by creating new circuits in their brain.
- Celebrate every step because success is in the trying.

Don't:

- Reveal your fears or disgust about the content of their obsession.
- Start too high on their hierarchy.
- Send them home to do ERP without practicing in session with them.
- Only attend to the exposure and not attend to their thoughts that maintain their fear. (See Chapter 7.)
- Reassure your client.
- Go down the rabbit hole of trying to figure out why they have this particular obsession.
- Teach relaxation techniques to help them decrease the anxiety connected to the exposure.

Chapter Highlights

- OCD preys on people's vulnerabilities and is the opposite of who they are.
- Create a safe and accepting environment for people to share their OCD fears/thoughts.
- Use the YBOCS to assess and develop a hierarchy for OCD.
- It is necessary to practice exposure therapy in session and out of session.
- Help your client develop ways to talk back to OCD.

TAKE THE NEXT STEP

List your own fears and obstacles related to working with clients who have OCD and find support from colleagues who treat OCD:

_____

_____

_____

_____

ANSWERS TO OCD LABELING EXERCISE

1. U
2. U
3. O
4. N
5. N
6. O
7. N
8. O
9. N
10. U
11. O

Chapter 11

Cognitive Behavioral Therapy for Panic Disorder

Most people are terrified the first time they have a panic attack. The overwhelming physical feelings can include a racing heart, sweating palms, nausea and diarrhea, and shaking and sweating. No wonder many people who have panic attacks have been to the emergency room thinking they are having a heart attack (Woud, Zhang, Becker, McNally, & Margraf, 2014).

Panic attacks can be either situational—meaning they occur in trigger situations, most commonly being away from a safe person or place or where escape is difficult, or spontaneous—out of the blue. Panic attacks can cause tremendous disability, as the sufferer avoids places and situations in order to prevent having those nasty feelings. The great news is that CBT helps 70–80% of clients become symptom-free (Craske & Barlow, 2014).

For example, Elizabeth worked with Dannie, who was 48 and started therapy for claustrophobia from being in parking garages or airplanes. She avoided her triggers as much as possible, and on the few occasions she had to fly, she took a benzodiazepine and held her husband's hand the whole time. Dannie was convinced the parking garages and airplanes were the problem. However, she did let Elizabeth know that part of her reason for seeking help was that, in the past few months, she had felt the same fear once when stopped at a red light in the rain, and another time when she was in a surface parking lot that she had parked in many times without fear. Dannie had been in therapy several times and her therapists had advised her to breathe deeply and find parking lots that were easier for her to use.

In their first session, Elizabeth explained the cognitive behavioral model to Dannie and explained that their goal was for her to live a full, rich life, but *not* that she would never have those terrifying feelings again. Once your brain knows how to have a panic attack, it will sometimes send out a panic reaction unexpectedly. All of the disability and most of the suffering comes from the fearful thoughts we add about the panic reaction, and the lengths we go to avoid triggering situations. Elizabeth let her know that, together, they needed to consider what was triggering her fear, and invited her to spend a week recording every time she had anxious feelings.

Dannie had a great life, except that she was quite ashamed of her fear of parking garages and airplanes, and she embraced CBT even though it was so different from what she had experienced with her previous therapists. When she returned for a second session, she had many other situations recorded as causing anxiety and some spontaneous panic as well. She recognized that the fear she felt was truly of the panic itself.

As with all work with anxious clients, be sure you start from a position of empathy with the client about how horrible they feel, and how much the problem is disturbing their life. Ask them to consider if anything they have done up until now has really worked—likely it has not, or they would not be there with you. Try to turn that frustration to a willingness or curiosity about trying a new approach. Having an attitude of curiosity about panic will be a big help with making the enormous transition you are going to ask for in their thoughts and actions toward panic.

AGORAPHOBIA

Many clients with panic disorder will be like Dannie, but some are much more severely disabled by anxiety and virtually homebound. Secure video sessions (teletherapy) can be the only way for some clients to get help if anxiety prevents them from leaving their home. For example, Evelyn, who was 25, and her husband lived with her parents due to her anxiety. Her husband left every day to go to work at a 9–5 job, but the family had staggered schedules so that someone was always home with Evelyn. She was never alone in the house. She left the house with one of her parents or her husband only in the evening after traffic had abated, so if she felt panicky, she could quickly return home. In fact, the only stores she would go to were ones where there was no traffic light between the store and her home. In stores, she went in for one or two items and quickly returned to the car while her family member waited in line to pay.

Evelyn was a smart woman who had gone to college online. She had landed a job as an editor and worked remotely from home. The complicated way that Evelyn and her family had learned to cope with her serious disability amazed us.

DEVELOPING A THERAPEUTIC ATTITUDE: BRING IT ON!

Panic disorder is all about fear of the feelings during a panic attack. In order to get well, clients have to practice bringing on the very feelings they fear. This is a radical shift in the way most clients with panic have been managing their anxiety. Help them see you are cultivating an attitude of bringing on panic. This will help free them from the prison they have been in as they have run in fear from these feelings.

It's really the same as all the other ways you have worked with your clients, but with panic disorder it is especially important to intentionally create the same bodily sensations they have with panic attacks. We call this interoceptive exposure. The intent is to trigger physiological symptoms of panic so that the client can restructure their cognitions around the sensations. This will help them to stay with the symptoms rather than resisting or avoiding. Hyperventilation is the fastest route to bringing on a panic attack. Keep a supply of straws in your office so you will be ready for interoceptive exposure with your clients. To trigger a panic attack using straw breathing, put the straw between your lips, and breathe quickly in and out only through the straw. Do not open your mouth or breathe through your nose for 15 seconds, 30 seconds, or one minute.

Elizabeth practiced straw breathing with Dannie at her second session. Elizabeth always needs to explain to clients that she herself gets panic attacks, too, so that she is just as likely as they are to have a panic attack while they practice. Some clients are horrified to think that she would subject herself to a panic attack for them. It's a great teaching moment—her panic attacks have never become panic disorder, because she always knew what they were and never backed away from the experience—Elizabeth feels she is an example of how well prevention works, since she learned about anxiety as a child before she had any symptoms. In sessions, she welcomes the chance to practice with her clients and trigger her own panic.

Dannie was very ready to get over her panic disorder. She had lived her whole adult life with this fear, but other than that she had a happy life. In comparison, Evelyn needed weekly sessions for two months before she was ready to bring on a panic attack in a session.

INTEROCEPTIVE EXPOSURE—BEHAVIORAL CHANGE

Dannie did straw breathing with Elizabeth for 30 seconds at her request, and she had fewer symptoms than Elizabeth did. They talked over their physical feelings for a few minutes, as well as what they were thinking when the panic symptoms arose. Then they did it again for a minute.

This was all a revelation to Dannie. In all her years of suffering, she had never realized that (1) the panic attacks were not dangerous and (2) she didn't have to run from them in fear. There are more exposures you and your clients can do together or assign as homework to bring on panic feelings.

Interoceptive Exposure

NOT ENOUGH AIR

Over-breathe: Breathe forcefully, fast and deep (1 min)

Breathe through a straw: hold your nose and breathe through the straw (2 min)

Hold your breath (30 sec)

HEART BEATING

Run in place quickly on the spot (2 min)

Lift your knees high (2 min)

Step up and down on a stair—hold onto rail for balance (1 min)

DIZZINESS

Spin while sitting in an office chair (1 min)

As fast as you can, spin around while standing up—make sure to leave yourself enough space and have a place to sit afterwards (30 sec)

HEAD RUSH

Put your head between your legs then sit up quickly (1 min)

Lie down and relax for at least 1 minute; then sit up quickly

UNREALITY

Stare at yourself in a mirror (2 min)

Concentrate hard without blinking (2 min)

Stare at a blank wall—concentrate hard without blinking (1 min)

Stare at a fluorescent light and then try to read something (1 min)

YOUR TURN

How do you feel about doing interoceptive exposures with your clients? If you are struggling to expose yourself to these unpleasant feelings or feel like you are being mean to your client by making them go through this, consider getting some support from a clinician who has done this before.

_____

_____

_____

_____

IDENTIFYING AND ELIMINATING SAFETY BEHAVIORS

As with all anxiety disorders, clients typically have been engaging in some type of safety behavior in order to manage their distress level. However, as you have seen, safety behavior only serves to continually reinforce the problems with anxiety by implying to the client that they cannot handle a situation without that safety behavior. For example, Dannie felt she could only fly if she took a benzodiazepine and held her husband's hand. Evelyn felt she could only go into a store if she knew she could leave in a few moments and not have to wait in line to check out. It's really clear with these examples how safety behaviors lock a client into dependence and disability.

Sure, Dannie was able to fly and Evelyn did go into stores, but they were only able to do those things with their safe people and so were dependent on an ongoing basis. For both women, safety behavior was just one more part of the limitation to their freedom that panic had created. Some examples of safety behaviors are: eating only certain foods; carrying a cell phone; meeting certain people; going to certain places; and sitting in a certain place in a car or building. These are only a few of the many ways clients with panic create false safety. It may be helpful to write a list of safety behaviors and then gradually remove them according to the ability of your client.

YOUR TURN

Think of a client with panic attacks that you treated. List the safety behaviors they engaged in:

_____

_____

_____

_____

WAYS TO TALK BACK TO PANIC—COGNITIVE RESTRUCTURING

The cognitive component to getting well from panic is very important—in fact, behavioral treatment alone is not considered effective therapy (Pompoli et al., 2016). It is vitally important to help your client reframe panic as distressing, but not dangerous. Use the metaphor of the false alarm, or the smoke detector going off when the pizza gets burned from Chapter 7. It's a normal bodily reaction, but to a false alarm since there is no current danger.

Help your client work at bossing back the anxiety—"I don't like this feeling. Bring more! I'm going to go live my life while you do the worst you can, anxiety. You can't stop me." For many clients, this ends up being paradoxical—the more they chase the symptom of panic, the less they experience panic. Some clients, of course, will still have quite a bit of panic, and that is not a failure. It may be that the addition of medicine like an SSRI will make a major difference in the anxiety they are experiencing, so consider medication for clients who are working hard, but still experiencing a lot of panic attacks (Payne et al., 2016).

Chapter Highlights

- Panic attacks are intense, and avoidance and safety-seeking behavior can cause significant suffering and disability.
- CBT for panic disorder includes understanding the psychology of panic and adopting a new attitude—bring it on!
- Interoceptive behavior is useful to practice the unpleasant bodily sensations of a panic attack.
- Use cognitive restructuring to help your client boss back anxiety.
- SSRI medicine may be used in addition to CBT.

TAKE THE NEXT STEP

Try our list of interoceptive exposures. They are vital for clients with panic, and helpful in a variety of other anxiety disorders, including emetophobia, or fear of vomiting. Record your experiences with them so you are ready for your next client who needs help with panic.

_____

_____

_____

_____

Chapter 12

Cognitive Behavioral Therapy for Worry

Generalized anxiety disorder (GAD) can be a challenging disorder to treat. People with this disorder are often called "worriers." These worries can feel relentless in their efforts to engage both our clients and ourselves in the therapy session. Stein and Sareen (2015), in their article "Generalized Anxiety Disorder," state that people usually present to their primary care physicians with this disorder, but rarely talk about worrying. Instead, they present with multiple somatic complaints. Chronic worry often leads to headaches and gastrointestinal distress.

We educate clients with this disorder by telling them that the purpose of worry is to protect them from negative experiences that lead to negative feelings in the future. They immediately connect to this definition and often go on to try to convince us why it is important for them to protect themselves from future harm.

WORRY IS A BRAIN GLITCH

If you remember from Chapter 4 about the anxious brain, it is our instinct to listen to our brain when it tells us of potential danger. Helping your client understand that this is a glitch in their brain trying to give them information about something in the future that hasn't happened is an important first step to treating worry. We often give clients articles to read about their disorder. One that we use for worriers is from *The Wall Street Journal*: "Worrying About the Future, Ruminating on the Past—How Thoughts Affect Mental Health" (Wang, 2015). The author of this article describes people who get thoughts stuck in their minds and find themselves ruminating. Wang also interviews experts who discuss ways to quiet the worry. You can share this article or use your own resources.

We also like to tell clients that worry is putting negative energy onto the person they are worrying about. This usually changes the conversation about the important function of their worry. Mothers don't want to add to the burden their children carry. After all, they are trying to protect them! Nonetheless, worry is a powerful force and often our clients find themselves caught up in the hamster wheel of these future thoughts.

Kimberly had a client who adored her teenage children. She took great care in protecting them. Her brain looked for any potential danger that may come to them. She listened to these danger signals and did everything she could to prevent these possible outcomes. As a result, her 16-year-old daughter had never been to the mall for fear she would be kidnapped. Her children had never been to a sleepover. Her college son lived at home and was not allowed to visit his friends at frat houses for fear he would get drunk and die of alcohol poisoning. Her children had to text her throughout the day to check in and let her know they were okay. Her husband spent his time with her reassuring her that she was a good parent and that their family would be okay. However, no amount of reassurance consoled her. Eventually, these worries extended past her children to her work as a teacher and to her friends.

In this chapter, we will look at ways to change our clients' relationships with worry, including playing with worry, developing exposures, using scripts, and challenging beliefs.

CBT Tips For Worry

- **Correct misinformation one time.** Worriers often spend time on issues that they are actually misinformed about. It is okay to provide accurate information, but don't get caught in the worry cycle by continuing the conversation.

- **Don't answer the questions or engage the content.** People with generalized anxiety disorder will often ask questions multiple times in an attempt to satiate their brain's need for certainty. If their questions are answered more than once, the anxiety circuit is connected and they will continue to feel the distress associated with uncertainty. Inform your client, as well as their family and friends, that engaging the content of their worry is not helpful and only serves to give power to their anxiety.

- **Don't engage the anxiety story.** A client with GAD spent two years telling her anxiety stories to her therapist, who diligently listened, reassured her, and engaged in problem-solving. The problems were always in the future. Consequently, they spent a lot of time talking about things that didn't exist and never happened.

- **Do see worry as a metaphor.** We teach clients to treat worry like white noise. It can be annoying, but does not need any response. We also ask them to practice with the car radio, tuning into the music and then tuning into their environment. Another way to understand this metaphor is to practice with young children in the back seat of the car. When they are whining or fighting, your client can see if they can tolerate it without saying anything to their children.

- **Practice a paradoxical approach.** Some clients benefit from setting aside 15 minutes to engage in intense worry. If worry pops up at other times, they can tell themselves that they will think about it during their "worry time." It can be challenging to purposefully worry for 15 minutes straight. This strategy may help them see the futility in coming up with worries for this predetermined length of time.

- **Look for opportunities to worry.** As you have learned throughout this workbook, the more clients can chase after their anxiety rather than being a victim of it, the better they get. Clients with GAD can engage in exposure therapy by looking for things to worry about. Some examples might be: "I could get in an accident today. I might be late to work. It's cloudy … maybe we'll get a storm and lose power. No one will like my dinner tonight." Chasing after worries puts your client in the driver's seat and helps them decide if they want to spend their time with these future-driven thoughts.

- **Labeling.** A helpful way to teach your clients to not engage the content of their worry is to have them label it "just a worry, period." When we teach this, we discuss the purpose of the word *just* and why there is a "period" at the end of the sentence.

YOUR TURN

Write your thoughts about why the labeling technique is helpful:

_____

_____

_____

PLAY WITH WORRY

In Chapter 6 on involving family members, we talked about the importance of changing the emotion. Anything they can do to shift their emotion by making fun of it or exaggerating it will take the power away from it. One way to do this is to have your clients write their worries on red sticky notes and put them on your wall. Have them fill up your wall, if possible. Then we go to work on finding simple ways to manage these worries and write them on different-colored sticky notes.

Some examples of helpful ways to talk back might be: breathe; I can handle that; I'm not in the future; I'm not having that conversation; just a worry. For each idea they come up with, they put the coping sticky note over the worry sticky note. Then have a conversation about how they felt putting the worries up versus putting the coping statements up.

YOUR TURN

Make a list of worries and coping statements, remembering to be realistic and factual in your statements, not positive.

Worry	Coping Statement
1.	
2.	
3.	
4.	
5.	
6.	

EXPOSURE TO WORRY

Therapists often struggle to figure out how to develop exposures to worries, because the nature of worry is that the fear doesn't actually exist in the present moment. Exposure scripts and visualization are helpful tools for worry.

Exposure scripts involve writing a story about worrying including the trigger, thoughts, feelings, and what they did about the worry. Then, have your client write the same story, but have them engage in coping strategies, including identifying the worry for what it is, engaging in healthy self-talk, and choosing their response. Have them read the following exposure script at least three times a day until your next session.

YOUR TURN

Write a worry script for something that you worry about.

···

Sample Worry Script

This is a sample of how to use a worry script. Read it several times a day, noticing how much you believe one scenario and how much you believe the other. Does it change?

WORRY SCENARIO

I wake up and feel a sensation in my throat. I begin to touch my neck, looking for something that explains this lump I feel. I notice a bit of a difference on the side of my neck where I feel the lump. I start to freak out. Do I have cancer? There must be something wrong with me or I wouldn't have noticed this. I can't wait for 8:00 a.m. when the doctor's office opens. I think I'm going to have a panic attack! Maybe I should contact the on-call doctor. I wake up my husband and tell him something is terribly wrong.

COPING SCENARIO

I wake up and feel a sensation in my throat. I begin to touch my neck and am unsure if I feel something different. I recognize that my anxiety is increasing. I tell myself that this may or may not be something to be concerned about, but I am not going to do anything with it now because I am not fully awake and I'm feeling anxious. I take a shower and eat some breakfast. My husband wakes up and I'm tempted to tell him my worry, but decide I won't say anything for 24 hours.

When 8:00 a.m. arrives, I want to call my doctor and make an appointment for today. I decide, instead, to wait three days before I make any call to my doctor to see how much anxiety is playing a role in this. Once my anxiety calms down, my body may be able to take care of this on its own. I will let myself do something about this only if it doesn't go away in three days or gets worse.

Your Worry Script

Use a worry script to help you consider other ways of looking at your fears. Read this script several times a day, noticing how much you believe one scenario and how much you believe the other. Does it change?

WORRY SCENARIO

_____

_____

_____

_____

_____

_____

COPING SCENARIO

_____

_____

_____

_____

_____

_____

_____

VISUALIZATION

Visualization can help your client develop tolerance to the feelings, sensations, and thoughts associated with worry. In session, have your client imagine their worst fear. Tell them to visualize as much of it as possible, including who is there, what they are thinking and feeling, as well as any sensations they may have access to. Now ask them to practice tolerating these images by becoming an observer of them. Help them to notice their experience without connecting to the content of the worry. Have them practice this each day at home.

BELIEFS ABOUT WORRY

Again, people who worry often believe that it is important to continue to worry to prevent bad things from happening. This is because they have not developed the ability to handle difficult events and emotions. It will be important for them to both change their beliefs about their thoughts, as well as practice experiencing difficult emotions and handling them.

The client whose worry greatly impacted her and her entire family is living a healthier life with her anxiety. She is able to go out at night without someone being with her. Her daughter goes to the mall and to movies with her friends. Her husband no longer reassures her, instead saying, "That is your anxiety. I won't talk to anxiety, but I will take a walk with you." Her kids are graduating and going away to college. She knows that worry will be a part of her life, but she no longer believes its catastrophic messages and works hard not to act on her fears.

The following are typical beliefs worriers have about their thoughts. Your work is to begin to challenge these thoughts using Socratic questioning.

1. Every thought is worth thinking about.
2. Every thought has meaning.
3. It's important to know where these thoughts come from.
4. I am responsible for my thoughts.
5. If I can't keep bad thoughts away, there is something wrong with me.
6. Not being certain signals danger.
7. Not remembering is unsafe.
8. In order to be happy, I must not have unwanted thoughts.
9. Ignoring thoughts is unhealthy.

YOUR TURN

Develop a Socratic question to challenge each belief listed above:

1. _____

2. _____

3. _____

4. _____

5. _____

6. _____

7. _____

8. _____

9. _____

Chapter Highlights

- Negative, repetitive thinking, or GAD, is an often underdiagnosed and poorly-treated disorder.
- GAD can leave people feeling that they and their families' lives are at the mercy of their ability to prevent bad things from happening.
- Worrying can consume enormous amounts of time, disrupt sleep, and leave people feeling emotionally and physically exhausted.
- The key to treating worry is to increase the ability to tolerate uncertainty and distress.

TAKE THE NEXT STEP

How do you discuss worry with your clients?

_____

_____

_____

_____

How much do you believe that worrying is helpful?

_____

_____

_____

_____

Do you feel confident helping your client to challenge their beliefs about worry?

_____

_____

_____

_____

If not, what can you do to practice this skill? Who can you go to for support/consultation?

_____

_____

_____

_____

_____

_____

What are some ideas you have to expose your client to uncertainty and distress?

_____

_____

_____

_____

_____

_____

Chapter 13

Termination and Relapse Prevention

Treatment termination ideally starts at the very first session when you acknowledge with your client that your goal is to work yourself out of a job. CBT is a short-term therapy. We want our clients to live full, rich lives without limitations due to anxiety or OCD once they complete therapy. This does not mean, however, that we are waiting for our clients to have no further anxiety or OCD symptoms before we complete our work!

We are training them to be their own self-help therapist and to be able to weather the likely ups and downs of anxiety and OCD. Just like handling any other type of chronic health problem, this is not a life sentence or unreasonable. Anxiety and OCD are manageable, and in many cases symptoms will go away, sometimes for long periods of time. However, setbacks are not only possible but likely, so it's important to normalize the ongoing nature of anxiety and OCD as part of treatment termination and relapse prevention.

As therapists, we get attached to our clients. We love hearing their successes and the growth that comes with the new lives they create that are no longer focused on anxiety. This makes it hard to say goodbye to some clients. Research shows us that the better the empathetic connection between client and therapist, the better the client will do in CBT. Because we are empathetic with our clients, we get attached. These feelings are important to acknowledge. Part of being a good CBT therapist is letting our clients go when they are ready (Teding van Berkhout & Malouff, 2016).

It was very hard to say goodbye to David, who was 18 and headed off to spend a summer in Europe before starting college in another state. We had worked together longer than with most clients, for about two years, because David was not only struggling with OCD, but his parents unexpectedly got divorced in his junior year. Before he began treatment, David spent hours every day talking to his girlfriend and best friend about how he could know he was alive, and other existential topics. Though he was smart and had done well in school before the start of his OCD symptoms, his grades were low because he had trouble starting and completing each assignment. He typically slept only a few hours a night because ending the day was so difficult for him. David's parents were preoccupied with their own changing lives and were only infrequently involved with David's treatment.

When starting work with clients who are severely disabled with anxiety or OCD, it can be hard to imagine we are working ourselves out of a job, and at the beginning, it was even hard to imagine David would be able to go away to college. In treatment, he was extremely successful in recognizing the way OCD hijacked his thoughts and kept him from completing one activity or thought before moving on to another. He became adept at saying to himself, "No choice, I have to move on even though it doesn't feel right." Medicine was also very important in his recovery.

YOUR TURN

Have you had a client it was hard to say goodbye to?

_____

_____

_____

WELLNESS FORMULA

Living a full, productive life involves developing a wellness formula, something that many people with anxiety don't have as they struggle with overwhelming symptoms. Wellness formulas involve exercise, healthy eating, sleep, work or volunteer activities, hobbies, and family and friendships. Take time in a session with your client to review these topics and set manageable goals for making changes where the two of you (and sometimes family or coaches) identify difficulties.

As with all our work, identify goals together, and set realistic, measurable steps. This can be an ongoing process for people who have been living very restricted lives. Annie, a 30-year-old woman, lived alone, walked to and from work and spent all her time alone. She was caught up in OCD cleanliness and safety rituals. Getting a companion animal, a cat, was a huge step for her and an important bridge to beginning to take time to have friendships.

SETBACKS INTO SPRINGBOARDS

Successful treatment involves learning to weather setbacks. Few people with anxiety and OCD will leave treatment symptom-free and never have another moment with anxiety. Especially in times of stress or with changes in life stages, anxiety will often find an opportunity to reappear. When your client starts a session with an update that they had unexpected difficulty, remember to reframe this for your client as an opportunity to strengthen their resilience while they are still in therapy!

Your client will typically be feeling bad about this setback and bad about telling you. This is a great trick that anxiety plays—focusing on this bad time and adding feelings of shame and failure. Have your client notice this is another automatic thought, and try to find a rational or neutral response: "I'm glad this happened while I'm still seeing my therapist so we can talk this over. I know that anxiety will come and go in my life; it's good to learn how to manage tough days or situations. I'm not a failure because I had a tough day. One tough day or situation does not make treatment a failure."

Sometimes a setback means it's a good idea to go back a step in treatment. You will look at your notes and your client will look at their notebook—when were things okay? Negative attention bias can make setbacks feel like they have lasted a lot longer than they have, especially because often clients will give up on the new exposures and behaviors they had learned. Try to go back and work on the last homework assignment that was successful. Remember that this setback offers the opportunity to learn something new about anxiety and therefore can be a springboard to new success—taking on new goals, trying new exposures, and learning more about mindfulness can all be next steps after a setback, but it rarely looks that way at first. Helping your client learn this new way of looking at stumbling will set them up for success after treatment.

Help your client develop a plan to manage setbacks by having them write answers to the following questions in their notebook:

- What triggered this setback?
- Did I change any of my behaviors? (stop exposure, get less sleep, etc.)
- What negative automatic thoughts do I have?
- What rational or neutral thoughts can I try instead?
- What exposures/healthy behaviors can I return to?
- Whom can I turn to for support?

RELAPSE PREVENTION—RED FLAGS

The goal is to prevent a setback from becoming a full relapse into the same problems they originally had with anxiety or OCD. Before terminating therapy, make a simple plan for relapse prevention, and have your client label it in their notebook with a red sticker. Red flags are the behaviors, moods, and attitudes that signal a return of anxiety and a likelihood of relapse. They are red flags to signal a need for action. Like the rest of treatment, red flags are specific for each client. Here are a few to give you an idea what these look like.

Annie's Red Flags

- Sleeping more than nine hours three days in a row.
- Not doing exposures two days in a row.
- Avoiding talking to people at work two days in a row.
- Missing work.

David's Red Flags

- Use mood app and track mood every Sunday, watch for low mood two weeks in a row.
- Going off my SSRI without talking to my doctor.
- Engaging my friends in long, abstract, intense conversations.
- Not getting work done on time.
- Not getting at least five hours of sleep a night for two nights.
- Not going to class.

Notice that these goals are specific, and, other than missing work or class—which are big red flags since they are very important and only disrupted by serious anxiety or OCD—they have to occur more than once to be considered red flags. In other words, everyone can have a bad day, and that isn't a red flag!

YOUR TURN

Which are red flags? (Answer is at the end of this chapter)

1. Calling in sick to work/skipping classes.
2. Missing a planned workout because a friend came to town for a visit.
3. Drinking a soda with caffeine and having a panic attack.
4. Cancelling plans with friends.
5. Getting angry or irritable with many people over several days.
6. Not doing planned anxiety practice because it is too hard.
7. Returning to former ways of avoiding anxiety.

TREATMENT TERMINATION

As mentioned, David had to terminate treatment because he was going to be traveling in Europe and then going to college in another state. He agreed to make an appointment at his college mental health center to ensure that he would have a therapist to work with if he needed help. No doubt, he will have moments when he does need help in the future, but even if we had not had the deadline that we did, David was ready to terminate treatment because he had been through several setbacks and had come through stronger.

David found great comfort in learning about the stories of other people with OCD, and found the International Obsessive Compulsive Foundation (www.iocdf.com) to be a particularly useful resource. He had achieved his goals and was living a rich, full life. Moreover, he knew exposure was a daily part of his life forever, as his symptoms came back whenever he missed a day. He was ready for the adventure he had planned and for the next stage of his life.

SIGNS THAT A CLIENT IS READY TO TERMINATE

- Achieved goals.
- Used CBT techniques in a new situation.
- New interests and activities in place of time spent on anxiety or OCD.
- Rich, full life.

We don't know the follow-up to David's story and that's the way it should be. We were part of that chapter and then he went on to live his own life. His successes are his own. We do know from other anxious clients and our own personal experience that CBT for anxiety and OCD has benefits far beyond the specific topics we work on at any given time. Life is unpredictable, and having the ability to tolerate uncertainty helps us to enjoy the wonderful things in life while managing the difficult, wherever our path leads.

Chapter Highlights

- Empathy leads to strong connections between clinician and client—it can be hard to say goodbye.
- Setbacks are opportunities for springboards ahead in treatment and life.
- Review wellness plan with clients.
- Set up red flags to warn of relapse.
- Remember that exposures are an ongoing part of life.
- Make a plan for when to seek therapy again.

TAKE THE NEXT STEP

Consider one client who might be ready for treatment termination and bring the topic up in a session. How did it go?

_____

_____

_____

_____

ANSWER TO RED FLAG EXERCISE

1. Calling in sick to work/skipping classes.

4. Cancelling plans with friends.

5. Getting angry or irritable with many people over several days.

6. Not doing planned anxiety practice because it is too hard.

7. Returning to former ways of avoiding anxiety.

References

Chapter 1

Beck, J. (2011). *Cognitive behavior therapy: Basics and beyond (second edition)*. New York: Guilford Press.

Burns, D. (2013, October 3). The ten worst errors therapists make, and how to avoid them. *Feeling good: A webpage of David D. Burns, MD* [Blog].

Clark, D.A. (1999). Anxiety disorders: Why they persist and how to treat them. *Behaviour Research and Therapy 37*, S5±S27.

Clark, D.A. & Beck, A. (2010). Cognitive theory and therapy of anxiety and depression: Convergence with neurobiological findings. *Trends in Cognitive Science*, 14(9), 418-24.

Otto, M., Smits, J., & Reese, H. (2004). Cognitive-behavioral therapy for the treatment of anxiety disorders. *Journal of Clinical Psychiatry*, 65(5), 34–41.

Jokić-Begić, N. (2010). Cognitive-behavioral therapy and neuroscience: Towards closer integration. *Psychological Topics*, 19(2), 235–254.

Chapter 2

Hara, K. M., Aviram, A., Constantino, M. J., Westra, H. A., & Antony, M. M. (2016). Therapist empathy, homework compliance, and outcome in cognitive behavioral therapy for generalized anxiety disorder: Partitioning within- and between-therapist effects. *Cognitive Behavior Therapy*, 15, 1–16.

Teding van Berkhout, E., & Malouff, J. M. (2016). The efficacy of empathy training: A meta-analysis of randomized controlled trials. *Journal of Counseling Psychology*, 63(1), 32–41. doi:10.1037/cou0000093. Epub 2015 Jul 20.

Szymanski, J. (2012). Using direct-to-consumer marketing strategies with obsessive-compulsive disorder in the nonprofit sector. *Behavior Therapy*, 43(2), 251–256. doi: 10.1016/j.beth.2011.05.005. Epub 2011 Jun 12.

Chapter 3

LeBeau, R. T., Davies, C. D., Culver, N. C., & Craske, M. G. (2013). Homework compliance counts in cognitive-behavioral therapy. *Cognitive Behaviour Therapy*, 42(3), 171–179.

Wolpe, Joseph (1969). *The practice of behavior therapy*, new york: pergamon press.

Chapter 4

Gold, A. L., Morey, R. A., & McCarthy, G. (2015). Amygdala–prefrontal cortex functional connectivity during threat-induced anxiety and goal distraction. *Biological Psychiatry*, 77(4), 394–403. doi: 10.1016/j.biopsych.2014.03.030. Epub 2014 Apr 19.

Van Apeldoorn, F. J., et al. (2008). Is a combined therapy more effective than either CBT or SSRI alone? Results of a multicenter trial on panic disorder with or without agoraphobia. *Acta Psychiatrica Scandinavica*, 117(4), 260–270.

Chapter 5

Gillihan, S. J., Williams, M. T., Malcoun, E., Yadin, E., & Foa, E. B. (2012). Common pitfalls in exposure and response prevention (EX/RP) for OCD. *Journal of Obsessive-Compulsive and Related Disorders*, 1(4), 251–257.

Goldin, P. R., Ziv, M., Jazaieri, H., Hahn, K., Heimberg, R., & Gross, J. (2013). Impact of cognitive behavioral therapy for social anxiety disorder on the neural dynamics of cognitive reappraisal of negative self-beliefs: Randomized clinical trial. *JAMA Psychiatry*, 70(10), 1048–1056. doi:10.1001/jamapsychiatry.2013.234

Salkovskis, P. (1991). The importance of behaviour in the maintenance of anxiety and panic: A cognitive account. *Journal of Behavioural and Cognitive Psychotherapy*, 19, 6–19.

Chapter 6

Lebowitz, E. R., Panza, K. E., Su, J., Bloch, M. H. (2012). Family accommodation in obsessive-compulsive disorder. *Expert Review of Neurotherapeutics*, 12(2), 229–238.

Chapter 7

McManus, F., Van Doorn, K., & Yiend, J. (2012). Examining the effects of thought records and behavioral experiments in instigating belief change. *Journal of Behavior Therapy and Experimental Psychiatry*, 43(1), 540–547. doi:10.1016/j.jbtep.2011.07.003

Schreiber, F., Heimlich, C., Schweitzer, C., & Stangier, U. (2015). Cognitive therapy for social anxiety disorder: The impact of the "self-focused attention and safety behaviours experiment" on the course of treatment. *Behavioural and Cognitive Psychotherapy*, 43(2), 158–166. doi:10.1017/ S1352465813000672

Weck, F., Neng, J., Richtberg, S., Jakob, M., & Stangier, U. (2015). Cognitive therapy versus exposure therapy for hypochondriasis (health anxiety): A randomized controlled trial. *Journal of Consulting and Clinical Psychology*, 83(4), 665–676. doi:10.1037/ccp0000013

Wilhelm, S., Berman, N. C., Keshaviah, A., Schwartz, R. A., & Steketee, G. (2015). Mechanisms of change in cognitive therapy for obsessive compulsive disorder: Role of maladaptive beliefs and schemas. *Behaviour Research and Therapy*, 65, 5–10. doi:10.1016/j.brat.2014.12.006

Chapter 8

Gillihan, S.J., Williams, M. T., Malcoun, E., Yadin, E., & Foa, E. B. (2012). Common pitfalls in exposure and response prevention (EX/RP) for OCD. *Journal of Obsessive-Compulsive and Related Disorders*, 1(4), 251–257.

Chapter 9

Higa-McMillan, C. K., Francis, S. E., Rith-Najarian, L., & Chorpita, B. F. (2016). Evidence base update: 50 years of research on treatment for child and adolescent anxiety. *Journal of Clinical Child & Adolescent Psychology*, 45(2), 91–113. doi: 10.1080/15374416.2015.1046177. Epub 2015 Jun 18.

James, A., Soler, A., Weatherall, R. (2005). Cognitive behavioural therapy for anxiety disorders in children and adolescents. *Cochrane Database of Systematic Reviews*,(4):CD004690.

Kendall, P. C., & Peterman, J. S. (2015). CBT for adolescents with anxiety: Mature yet still developing. *American Journal of Psychiatry*, 172(6), 519–530. doi: 10.1176/appi.ajp.2015.14081061

McLeod, B. D., Islam, N. Y., Chiu, A. W., Smith, M. M., Chu, B. C., & Wood, J. J. (2014). The relationship between alliance and client involvement in CBT for child anxiety disorders. *Journal of Clinical Child & Adolescent Psychology*, 43(5), 735–741. doi:10.1080/15 374416.2013.850699

Chapter 11

Craske, M.G. & Barlow, D.H. (2014). Panic disorder and agoraphobia. In Clinical Handbook of Psychological Disorders, Fifth Edition (pp. 1-61). D.H. Barlow (Ed.). Guilford Press: New York, New York.

Payne, L. A., White, K. S., Gallagher, M. W., Woods, S. W., Shear, M. K., Gorman, J. M., ... & Barlow, D. H. (2016). Second-stage treatments for relative nonresponders to cognitive behavioral therapy (CBT) for panic disorder with or without agoraphobia—continued CBT versus SSRI: A randomized controlled trial. *Depression and Anxiety*, 33(5), 392–399. doi:10.1002/da.22457. Epub 2015 Dec 10.

Pompoli, A., Furukawa, T. A., Imai, H., Tajika, A., Efthimiou, O., & Salanti, G. (2016). Psychological therapies for panic disorder with or without agoraphobia in adults: A network meta-analysis. *Cochrane Database of Systematic Reviews*, 13(4):CD011004. doi:10.1002/14651858. CD011004.pub2

Woud, M. L., Zhang, X. C., Becker, E. S., McNally, R. J., & Margraf, J. (2014). Don't panic: Interpretation bias is predictive of new onsets of panic disorder. *Journal of Anxiety Disorders*, 28(1), 83–87. doi:10.1016/j.janxdis.2013.11.008

Chapter 12

Stein, M., & Sareen, J. (2015). Generalized anxiety disorder. *New England Journal of Medicine*, 373, 2059–2068.

Wang, S. (2015, August 10). Worrying about the future, ruminating on the past: How thoughts affect mental health. *Wall Street Journal*.

Chapter 13

Teding van Berkhout, E., & Malouff, J. M. (2016). The efficacy of empathy training: A meta-analysis of randomized controlled trials. *Journal of Counseling Psychology*, 63(1), 32–41. doi:10.1037/cou0000093. Epub 2015 Jul 20.

Recommended Reading

Anxiety and Depression Association of America. "Myth-conceptions," about anxiety. https://www.adaa.org/understanding-anxiety/myth-conceptions. (Some common myths vs. actual facts about anxiety disorders and effective treatment.)

Beck, A. T. (1976). *Cognitive therapies and emotional disorders.* New York: New American Library.

Beck, J. (2011). *Cognitive behavior therapy: Basics and beyond (second edition).* New York: Guilford Press.

Brantley, J. (2007). *Calming your anxious mind: How mindfulness and compassion can free you from anxiety, fear, and panic* (2nd ed.). Oakland, CA: New Harbinger Publications.

Burns, D. D. (1980). *Feeling good: The new mood therapy.* New York: New American Library.

Chansky, T. (2000). *Freeing your child from obsessive compulsive disorder.* New York: Crown Publishers.

Craske, M. G., & Barlow, D. H. (2014). *Panic disorder and agoraphobia.* In D. H. Barlow (ed.), *Clinical handbook of psychological disorders* (5th ed.), pp. 1–61. New York: Guilford Press.

Huebner, D. (2005). *What to do when you worry too much: A kid's guide to overcoming anxiety.* Washington, DC: Magination Press.

Kabat-Zinn, J. (2013). *Full catastrophe living: Using the wisdom of your body and mind to face stress, pain, and illness* (rev. ed.). New York: Bantam Books.

Morrow, K. (2011). *Face it and feel it: 10 simple (but not easy) ways to live well with anxiety.* Published by Kimberly Morrow.

Orsillo, S., & Roemer, L. (2011). *The mindful way through anxiety: Break free from chronic worry and reclaim your life.* New York: Guilford Press.

Pittman, C. (01/09/2013). Why me? Explaining anxiety in the brain. https://www.adaa.org/living-with-anxiety/ask-and-learn/webinars.

Seif, M., & Winston, S. (2014). *What every therapist needs to know about anxiety disorders.* New York: Routledge.

Wagner, A. P. (2013). *Up and down the worry hill: A children's book about obsessive-compulsive disorder and its treatment.* n.p.: North Carolina: Lighthouse Press.

Wilson, R. (2009). *Don't panic* (3rd ed.). New York: Harper Collins.

Wilson, R. (2016). *Stopping the noise in your head: The new way to overcome anxiety and worry.* Deerfield Beach, FL: Health Communications, Inc.

Young, J. E., Klosko, J. S., & Beck, A. T. (1994). *Reinventing your life: The breakthrough program to end negative behavior and feel great again.* New York: Plume.

Websites

10% Happier: http://www.10percenthappier.com/mindfulness-meditation-the-basics/

Anxiety and Depression Association of America (ADAA): http://www.adaa.org

Buddhify: app for mindfulness.

Current guidelines about medicines for anxiety disorders in adults and children: https://www.nimh.nih.gov/health/topics/anxiety-disorders/index.shtml

Headspace—Meditation Made Simple: https://www.headspace.com/

International Obsessive Compulsive Foundation (YBOCS): http://www.iocdf.org

Reducing "Family Accommodation Behaviors": https://iocdf.org/families/

Made in the USA
Coppell, TX
16 September 2021